# THE CONVERSATIONAL BIBLE

## THE NEW TESTAMENT
### IN STORY FORM

ANGELA SCOTT

AMBASSADOR INTERNATIONAL
GREENVILLE, SOUTH CAROLINA & BELFAST, NORTHERN IRELAND
www.ambassador-international.com

# The Conversational Bible

The New Testament in Story Form

© 2016 by Angela Scott
All rights reserved

Hardcover ISBN: 978-1-62020-557-0
Paperback ISBN: 978-1-64960-495-8
eISBN: 978-1-62020-481-8

Holman Christian Standard Bible® Copyright © 1999, 2000, 2002, 2003, 2009 by Holman Bible Publishers. Used with permission by Holman Bible Publishers, Nashville, Tennessee. All rights reserved.

Cover Design & Typesetting by Hannah Nichols
Ebook Conversion by Anna Riebe Raats

AMBASSADOR INTERNATIONAL
Emerald House
411 University Ridge, Suite B14
Greenville, SC 29601, USA
www.ambassador-international.com

AMBASSADOR BOOKS
The Mount
2 Woodstock Link
Belfast, BT6 8DD, Northern Ireland, UK
www.ambassadormedia.co.uk

*The colophon is a trademark of Ambassador*

*For Mom and Dad*

———————————

Thank you: Jewel Hatch, a Sunday School teacher who planted deep seeds of faith when teaching mom to memorize Psalm 23 at five years of age; Dr. Richard Hipps, friend and former pastor; and the late Pastor Michael Shroyer, friend, children's ministry pastor, and former pastor.

*The one who believes in Me, as the Scripture has said, will have streams of living water flow from deep within him.*

—John 7:38, HCSB

# CONTENTS

| | |
|---|---|
| INTRODUCTION | 11 |
| THE BIRTH OF CHRIST | 13 |
| THE STAR IN THE EAST | 19 |
| THE BOYHOOD OF JESUS | 21 |
| JESUS AND JOHN THE BAPTIST | 25 |
| THE WOMAN AT THE WELL | 31 |
| JESUS BY THE SEA | 33 |
| JESUS HEALS THE SICK | 35 |
| JESUS DOES GOOD WORKS ON THE DAY OF REST | 37 |
| THE SERMON ON THE MOUNT | 41 |
| GOOD WORDS AND GOOD WORKS | 47 |
| JESUS AT THE SEASHORE | 51 |
| JESUS BRINGS THE DEAD TO LIFE | 57 |
| JESUS HEALS THE SICK | 61 |
| JESUS'S FORM CHANGED ON THE MOUNT | 63 |
| THE GOOD SAMARITAN | 65 |
| MARTHA AND MARY | 67 |
| THE MAN BORN BLIND | 69 |
| JESUS THE GOOD SHEPHERD | 71 |
| LAZARUS BROUGHT TO LIFE | 73 |
| THE FEAST AND THOSE WHO WERE INVITED TO ATTEND | 77 |

| | |
|---|---|
| THE PRODIGAL SON | 79 |
| THE PHARISEE AND THE PUBLICAN | 81 |
| BABES BROUGHT TO JESUS | 83 |
| THE FEAST OF THE PASSOVER – THE SUPPER AT BETHANY | 85 |
| PARABLES | 89 |
| THE LORD'S SUPPER | 95 |
| JESUS IN GETHSEMANE | 97 |
| THE JUDAS KISS | 99 |
| PETER DENIES JESUS | 101 |
| CHRIST GOES BEFORE PILATE | 103 |
| ON THE CROSS | 105 |
| JESUS LEAVES THE GRAVE | 111 |
| JESUS APPEARS TO MARY | 113 |
| STEPHEN IS KILLED BY STONING | 115 |
| PAUL'S LIFE, SHIPWRECK, AND DEATH | 117 |
| WHAT JOHN SAW WHILE ON THE ISLE OF PATMOS | 121 |
| THE GREAT WHITE THRONE | 123 |
| THE LAND OF LIGHT | 125 |
| INDEX OF ILLUSTRATIONS | 126 |
| BIBLIOGRAPHY | 127 |

# INTRODUCTION

*Most of the important things in the world have been accomplished by people who have kept on trying when there seemed to be no hope at all.*
—Dale Carnegie

*History of the New Testament in Words of One Syllable,* published in 1888, was hidden from today's readers except for a hardback copy given to me a few years ago from a cousin as a birthday gift. Reading about events in story form from New Testament Scripture intrigued me. The classic illustrations also gave me reason to pause. Long before learning how to read, sitting with the family Bible and looking at the full-page pictures was among my favorite things to do as a young child.

The copyright date of 1888 in Josephine Pollard's book intrigued me, almost as much as the New Testament stories. Compelled to answer "the call" from God to share these wonderful events in conversational story form with you, I understood He had chosen me for this task; however, I found myself giving God a similar excuse as Moses offered when he was called to serve God: "You don't understand, I stutter" (Exodus 4:10). I told God all of my excuses and emphasized my flaws rendering me inadequate for this assignment. I recalled the story of Noah's response to God when He had called him to "Build an ark in this dry land." My response, "I need a ruler to build a straight line." And so the excuses went on until I said yes to God.

Join me on this adventure to meet Jesus. It is my privilege to accompany you as you read these New Testament events and treasure the illustrations. Your life will never be the same when you listen for God's whisper to you.

The Nativity

# THE BIRTH OF CHRIST

The time was near for Jesus to come to the earth. God had told Adam and Eve of One who would save them from their sins. Moses, and all the seers and wise men, spoke of Him who was to give men new hearts and help them to lead new lives.

In the days of Herod, king of Judea, there was a priest named Zechariah. His wife's name was Elizabeth. They were both old, had led pure lives, and sought to keep God's laws. But they had no child.

One day when the priest Zechariah was in the house of God by one of the altars, an angel came and stood near him. When the priest saw the angel, he shook with fear.

But the angel said, "Fear not, Zechariah, for God will give you and your wife a son, and you will call his name John. He will be great in the sight of the Lord, will not drink wine nor strong drink, and will turn the hearts of men to the Lord their God."

Then Zechariah asked the angel, "But how will I know that these things will be?"

And the angel said to him, "I am the angel Gabriel, who stands near to God, and He has sent me to tell you this good news. And for your lack of faith, you will become silent, and speak not a word until the day that these things come to pass."

Now those who were in the courts of God's house thought it strange that Zechariah should stay so long at the altar where he burnt the incense.

When Zechariah came out, he could not speak to them but made them know by signs that he had seen a strange sight.

Six months later, God sent the angel Gabriel to the town of Nazareth to a young woman there whose name was Mary. She was a descendant of King David.

When Mary saw the angel, she was in great fear for she knew not why he had come. The angel said, "Fear not, Mary, for God has blessed you. You will have a son, and will call His name JESUS. He will be great and will be called the Son of God. God will make Him a king, and to His reign there will be no end."

Mary asked, "How can this be?"

The Annunciation

The angel told her that what might seem hard for her was not hard for God, who could do all things. The angel had told Elizabeth that she would have a son, and now God had sent word to Mary that she would have a son, and what God had said He would do.

Then Mary said, "Let the Lord's will be done," and the angel left her.

Mary immediately went to the land of Judah, to the house of Elizabeth and Zechariah, where she spent three months. Then she returned to her own home. Joseph was the name of Mary's husband; he was a Jew of King David's line too. They were both poor, and Joseph had to work hard at his trade. He was a carpenter.

God gave Zechariah and Elizabeth the son that He said they should have. When the child was eight days old, the friends and kinsfolk came to see the baby and to give him a name. Most of them said, "Call him Zechariah."

But Elizabeth said, "Not so. He will be called John."

They said, "There is none of your family called by this name," and made signs to the father that he should let them know by what name the child should be called.

Zechariah sat down and wrote, "His name is John," and the people all thought this strange, because he had not told them of the angel who had spoken to him in the house of God.

As soon as Zechariah wrote these words, his speech came back to him, and he gave praise and thanks to God. All the folks in that part of the land heard of these things, and they said, "What sort of a child will this be?" The boy grew tall and strong, and the Lord blessed him. He went out and dwelled in the woods and wastelands until he was a man, and it was time for him to preach to the Jews and to tell them of Jesus.

Now the king of Rome was called Caesar Augustus in the dialect of that land, and the Jews had to do just as he said. He made a law requiring the names of all the Jews be written in a book that it might be known what tribe they came from and what they were worth. With the names of the Jews in that book, it would be easy to count the number of Jews living in the land where Caesar Augustus had fought and won.

Each Jew was to go to that part of the land where his forefathers dwelled and have his name written in the book at that place.

So, as Joseph and his wife were of the house of David, they both set out for the town of Bethlehem, where David used to feed his sheep. The way was long, and when they came to the town they found a great crowd of folks there. There was no room for Joseph and Mary at the inn, and they knew no one at whose house they could stay.

As they went from place to place in search of a room, they came to a stable in which there was a great trough, or manger, full of hay, where the poor folks who came to town fed the animals on which they rode.

So Joseph and Mary made their home in this stable while they had to wait to have their names written down. While they were there, God gave to Mary the son that He said she should have.

As she had no fine, soft clothes to wrap the baby in, she took bands of cloth, put them around Him, and laid Him on the straw in the manger.

In those days, rich men kept large flocks of sheep and goats and had men watch them at night for fear that wild beasts would seize and kill them. The men who fed and took care of the sheep were called shepherds.

One night, as some shepherds were on the hills where they kept watch of their flocks, the angel of the Lord came down to them. And a bright light shone round them so that they were very afraid.

The angel said to them, "Fear not, for I bring you good news which will give joy to all the land. For Christ, the Lord, is born for you this day, in the town of Bethlehem, and He will save you from your sins. And this is the way you will know Him: 'You will find the babe wrapped in bands of cloth and lying in a manger.'"

When the angel had said this, there came, like a flash of light, a great host of angels who gave praise to God and sang, "Glory be to God on high, and on earth, peace and good will to men."

When the angels had left them, the shepherds said, "Let us go at once to Bethlehem and see these things of which the angel has told us."

The shepherds went with haste and found Mary and Joseph, and the babe that lay in the manger where the animals were fed. When the shepherds had seen the child, they went out and told what the angel had said to them. Those who heard were filled with awe, for it was the first time that such a thing had been done in the world. The strange news spread fast.

Mary told no one of the talk she had had with the angel, but thought much of these things, and took the best of care of the newborn babe. It did not seem as if it could be her own child.

Simeon in the Temple

When the babe was eight days old, His father and mother gave Him the name of Jesus, as the angel had bid them. They gave Him to the Lord; that is, they vowed to the priest that they would bring up the child to serve God and to lead a good life. Though He was the Son of God, He was sent to earth to teach men what they ought to do.

Now there was a man in Jerusalem whose name was Simeon. He was a good man and did what was right. For years he had been on the watch for one of whom the seers had told, and who was to save men from their sins.

It was made known to Simeon in a dream that he should not die until he had seen this King of kings and Lord of lords.

Simeon was a priest in the house of God, and when Joseph and Mary brought in the child Jesus, he took Jesus up in his arms and blessed God, saying, "Now, Lord, your words have come true, and I can die in peace, for I have seen Him who is to be the light of the world and to save men from their sins!"

Joseph and Mary did not know what to make of this strange speech. The priest blessed them and gave the child back to his mother and told her of some of the great things He would do when He grew up to be a man.

There was a woman named Anna, a daughter of Phanuel of the tribe of Asher, who kept all the fasts and served God night and day. She was forty-four years old and could foretell what was to take place, and her fame was great. She came into the house of God while Simeon yet spoke, gave thanks to the Lord, and told of him who was to come to save the Jews and to give them back their rights.

Then Mary and Joseph returned to their own home in Nazareth. The child grew and was strong and wise, and God blessed Him from day to day.

The Guiding Star

## THE STAR IN THE EAST

In those days God spoke to men by strange signs, and wise people were all the time on the watch for them. They had read in their old books of a star that was to shine with a bright light, and each night they would raise their eyes to the sky in hopes that they might see this sign that would bring hope and joy to the whole race of Jews. But years and years had gone by, and the Jews had no land of their own and were as slaves to Caesar of Rome. Herod, their king, was most harsh to them, for he had skill in the use of a sword but not in the use of kind words or good deeds.

One night as a wise man lay on the roof of his house with his gaze fixed on the great broad sky, he cried with joy when he saw a new star of such size that all the rest of the stars grew dim and small. It was as if the sun had burst through a dark cloud and the dawn of day had arrived early, because the whole East was full of light from the long rays of this new star.

The star seemed to move, and its rays to point all one way. The wise men who had seen it knew that the light for which they had looked and prayed so long had come. They set out at once with the star to guide them, and they took rich gifts with them. Each night it shone in the sky, and led them on and on until they came to Jerusalem. They said to those they met there, "Where is He that is born to be King of the Jews? For we have seen His star in the East and have come to kneel down at His feet."

When Herod heard of these things, and that they spoke of Jesus as King, he was very afraid that he might lose his throne. So Herod sent for his chief priests and scribes that they might tell him where Christ should be born. They read from their old books that it had been foretold that Christ should be born in Bethlehem.

Then Herod sent for the wise men and told them to go to Bethlehem and to search for the young child. "When you find Him," said the king, "bring me word that I too may fall down at His feet and give Him praise."

But Herod did not mean to give Christ praise; his plan was to put the child to death just as soon as he could find out where the child was.

When the king had ceased to speak, the wise men from the East departed from Jerusalem and went on their way to Bethlehem. The star led them on and on and was like the face of a friend. A small, still voice seemed to say to them: "Come! Come! Come!" It drew them so that they would have gone to the ends of the earth.

When the wise men came to Bethlehem, the star that had led them stood still in the sky, right over the place where the young child was. When they went into the house, they saw the young child with Mary, His mother, and they fell on their knees and bowed down to Him as if He were a king. They brought Him gifts of great worth, gold, myrrh, and rich gums and spice that can be found only in those lands in the far East.

Wise Men Bringing Gifts

God spoke to them in a dream and told them not to go back to Herod, so the wise men went home a different way than they had come.

When Herod found out that the wise men had not done as he asked them, he was in a great rage and sent men to Bethlehem to slay all the children there who were two years old or younger. Then, Herod was sure that Jesus would be slain.

But before Herod's men came, God spoke to Joseph in a dream and said, "Rise and take your wife and your son, flee into Egypt, and stay there until I bring word to you; Herod will seek Jesus to kill Him."

So Joseph did as the Lord told him and took his wife and child out of Bethlehem by night and went to dwell in the land of Egypt.

But when Herod was dead, God spoke to Joseph again in a dream and told him to take his wife and son and return to the land of Israel, for the man was dead who sought to kill the young child. Joseph did as the angel told him, and he and his wife and child went and dwelled in Nazareth.

## THE BOYHOOD OF JESUS

It was in the first month of the year that God brought the Jews out of Egypt and led them through the Red Sea. He made it a law that in the first month of each year they should all meet at one place and bring the young lambs, calves, and the first fruits of the field, giving thanks to God in the way they had been taught. They were to do this all the days of their life. This feast, which was to last not quite two months, was known as the Feast of the Weeks. There were days they were to fast and days they were to feast. They were to call to mind they were once slaves, and that God had set them free, and with glad hearts praise and bless His great name.

The place where the Jews now met was at Jerusalem, and Jesus was twelve years old when He went up for the first time with Joseph and Mary to keep the Feast of the Weeks.

There was a great crowd and friends to meet and talk with, and it must have been a hard task to keep track of the young folks who found so much to see and to hear that was new and strange.

When the days of the feast were at an end, Joseph and Mary set out for their home in Nazareth. They had gone out with a band of friends and folks from the same town and were to return in the same way. It was not safe for them to go by themselves, for there were wastelands to cross where bands of thieves lay in wait for a chance to rob and to kill those who came their way.

Some people rode on mules, some on horseback, and some had to walk all the way. Jesus was not with Joseph and Mary, but they thought He must be with some of the friends or family. But when at the end of a day's ride Jesus didn't come to them, Mary and Joseph looked for Him in the groups of friends and family where there were lads of his own age.

And when they did not find Him, they went back to Jerusalem and looked for Him with hearts full of grief, for they knew not what harm might have come to Him.

For three days they went from house to house and through the lanes and streets, but they could see no signs of the boy they had lost.

At the end of that time, they went into the house of God—it may have been to pray that their child might be found—and there a strange sight met their gaze.

Jesus sat in the midst of the wise men, whose place it was to teach and to preach to those who came up to the feasts, and the old men bent their heads to hear what the young lad had to say. It was the first time the old men had met with one so young in years who was so wise in speech, and they felt in their hearts that He must have been taught of God.

Jesus in the Temple

When Joseph and Mary saw Jesus, they were struck speechless and the only thing they could do was stare as if it was a scene in a dream. Then Mary said, "My son, why did you anger us like this? We have looked for you with sad hearts."

Jesus said, "Why did you look for me? Don't you understand that I must do the work that my Father has sent me to do?"

Joseph and Mary did not know what He meant by those words or that God had sent Jesus on earth to teach men how to read the word of God with comprehension and understand how God saves their souls from death.

Jesus went back to Nazareth with Joseph and Mary and was a good son to them. He grew wise and tall, was blessed of God, and won the hearts of all who were near Him, for they saw in Him much to love.

It was not known that He was the Son of God, and He made friends by His own sweet ways because He was poor.

Nothing was heard or known of Jesus for some years, and we are led to think that He was taught how to use the axe, saw, and level, and to work at the same trade his father did. This gave Him a chance to see how folks lived and to use His eyes and ears as He went forth to teach, tell them of their sins, and show them how vile they were.

This part of the life of Jesus—of which not a word is told in the New Testament—is to teach us to stay in the place where God has put us and to do our work there in the best way we know how.

Jesus was at school then, just as boys and girls in these days go to school and strive to grow wise and to fit themselves for the work they are to do in the world. Though He was to be a king, He did not put on airs or sit and fold His hands and bid those that were near to wait on Him and be at His beck and call. No! He was born and brought up with poor folks to teach us that Jesus is more at home with the poor than He is with the rich; to be Christlike we must seek to please God, to do His will, to put down pride, and keep sin out of our hearts.

John the Baptist

## JESUS AND JOHN THE BAPTIST

You have been told that John went out into the woods and wastelands while he was still quite a young man. He fed on locusts and wild honey, and his clothes were made of the skin of the camel with the long rough hair on the outside.

The time had now come for him to go out in the world to tell of Jesus and command men to repent from their sins and walk in the right path.

He went to a place near the Jordan River and crowds came there to hear him. He told them that he had been sent to warn them to flee from the wrath to come. He said they must not think they would be saved because they were sons or heirs of good men who had served God and died in the faith. He told them that each person should be like a tree and to stand in his place and bring forth fruit, to serve God in the best way that he could. Each tree, said John, which does not bring forth good fruit is cut down and cast into the fire.

When those who heard him felt a great hate for sin and a strong wish to lead good lives, they spoke to John, and he led them down to the Jordan River where they were dipped in the stream.

Now water will wash the stains from our clothes and cleanse our skin, but it will not wash our sins away. To do this, we must have Christ in our hearts, and John said to these Jews, "I indeed baptize you with water, but He who is to come after me, and who is greater than I, will baptize you with fire."

That meant that Jesus would be in their hearts like a fire, to burn up all that was bad, as they burned the chaff that was blown loose from the wheat.

Then Jesus came from His home in Nazareth to have John baptize Him in Jordan's stream. But John would not. He said there was more need that Jesus should baptize him. He felt that there was need to have his own sins washed away, but Jesus had no sins. "So why do you come to me?" asked John.

Jesus had come on the earth as a man to do God's will and to teach mankind how to walk in the right path and keep their hearts free from sin. He told John that all these things would be made plain to him some day, and it was right that he should baptize Him.

So John went with Jesus into the water and laid his hands on Jesus's head, as he had done to all the rest.

As Jesus went up out of the water there came a great light in the sky that took the form of a dove and came down and seemed to rest on Him. God's voice spoke out of the sky and said, "This is my dear Son, with whom I am well pleased."

Then Jesus went out into the wastelands and was there with no one near Him for more than a month. In all that time He ate no food, but spent the hours talking with God. At last He felt weak and faint and left the wastelands to go in search of something to eat.

The Baptism of Christ

Now there is a fiend in this world, as we all know, who has a dark heart and can take on all sorts of shapes. He came to Eve in the form of a snake. He tempts those to do wrong who have set out to do right, and we have to be on our guard all the time to watch and pray that we may be kept safe from him.

When this fiend saw Jesus on His way to give new hearts to men and to make them good and pure, the fiend thought he would try and put a stop to such work. So he went out to tempt Jesus with the same smooth voice in which he spoke to Eve.

Satan came to Jesus and said, "If you are the Son of God change those stones into bread, so that you can eat now that you are starving."

Jesus knew why Satan had come, and He told him that men should take more pains to do God's will than to get bread to eat. Next Satan took Jesus to Jerusalem and up to a high place where the house of God was built. He said to

Jesus, "If You are the Son of God, throw Yourself down, for it is said, He will give His angels charge to keep Him in all His ways. They will bear you up in their hands unless you dash against a stone.

Jesus told him that it was not right to go where it was not safe, just to test God.

Then Satan took Jesus up on a high mount, from where all the large towns in the lands and all their great wealth could be seen, and Satan said to Jesus, "All these will I give You for Your own if You will kneel down and worship me."

Jesus said to him, "Go from me, Satan, for it is written in God's Word, 'You will worship the Lord Your God and Him alone will you serve.'"

When Satan found that Jesus paid no heed to his words, he left Him, and angels came to wait on the Son of God.

In a short time, Jesus returned to the Jordan where John was, and when John saw Him, he said, "Behold the Lamb of God!"

He spoke of Jesus as the Lamb of God, for He was to be laid on the cross for the sins of men as the lamb was in those days laid on the altar.

Then Jesus set out to preach and to turn men from their sins. He went to Galilee. One day as He walked by the seashore, He saw two men cast their net into the sea. Their names were Andrew and Peter. Jesus said to them, "Come with me," and they left their nets at once that they might be near Him and learn of Him.

The next day Jesus saw two men whose names were James and John in a boat with their father. Their nets had broken, and they were in a rush to mend them so they could take in a large haul of fish. But Jesus spoke to James and John, and they left the boat at once and went with Him that He might teach them.

The next day Jesus spoke to Philip and Nathaniel, and they left their homes and went with Him.

When Jesus came to the town of Cana, He found quite a crowd there, for a wedding was to take place, and He and His mother had been invited to the feast. There was food to eat and wine to drink, but before the feast was over, all of the wine had been consumed. When Mary knew of it, she said to Jesus, "They have no wine." She asked those who were there to serve the guests to do just as Jesus told them.

Now there were in the house six large stone jars, such as the Jews kept for holding water. Jesus said to the men, "Fill the jars with water," and they filled them to the brim. He said to them, "Take some out now and bear it to the chief guest of the feast," and they did so; the water was changed into wine.

The chief guest did not know what Jesus had done, but when he had tasted some of the wine he sent for the bridegroom and said to him, "As a rule, those who give a feast set out the good wine first, and when the guests have had all they care for, they bring out the wine that is poor. But you have kept the good wine until now."

This was the first great sign Jesus gave of the power He had from on high. It was proof to those whose hearts were with Him that He was the Son of God.

The time of the Feast of Weeks was at hand, and Jesus went up to Jerusalem to keep it. In one of the courts were men who had brought their goods to the house of God to sell them to the Jews when they came up to the feast. When Jesus came to the place where these men were, the sight did not please Him. Jesus made a scourge, or whip of small cords, and drove them all out, with their flocks and their herds. He poured their gold and silver on the ground and said to those who sold doves, "Take them away; make not the house of God a place to buy and sell in."

While He was at the feast, crowds were drawn to Him and had faith in Him when they saw what wonders He could do. Nicodemus, one of the chief men of the Jews, came to Jesus in the night and said to Him, "We know that God has sent You to teach us what is right, for no man could do these wonders if God were not with Him."

Driving out the Sellers

Jesus told him that he must have a new heart, or he could not be a child of God.

Herod, who slew the babes of Bethlehem, was dead, but his son, also named Herod, ruled in that part of Galilee, and he was a bad man. He took his brother's wife from him and made her for his own wife. Her name was Herodias. When John the Baptist told Herod this was not right, Herod would have put John to death if he had dared. But he had heard John preach and knew that he was a good man. Yet to please Herodias, Herod seized John, bound him, and shut him up in jail.

While John was in jail, Herod, on his birthday, made a great feast for the lords and chief men of Galilee, and a young girl named Salome, who was Herodias's daughter, came and danced in their midst. Herod was so much pleased with her that he said, "Ask of me what you will, and you will have it, though it would be half of my realm."

Salome went to Herodias and said, "What will I ask?"

Herodias said to her, "Ask the king to cut off the head of John the Baptist and bring it to you here in a large dish."

Salome immediately returned to the king and said, "Give me, in a large dish, the head of John the Baptist."

Herod was grieved, but as he had sworn to give her what she asked for, and those who sat near had heard him, he felt bound to keep his word. So he sent one of his soldiers, who cut off John's head in the jail and brought it in a large dish to Salome, and she gave it to her mother.

When the friends of John heard of it, they came up and took his body without his head, laid it in a tomb, and went and told Jesus.

The Woman at the Well

# THE WOMAN AT THE WELL

One day, Jesus and His disciples came to the town of Sychar, near a well where all the folks came to get water. The sun was hot, and Jesus, tired from His long walk, sat down by this well to rest while His disciples went to the town to buy food.

A woman came from the town to draw water. She had led a life of sin and had no love for God in her heart. Jesus knew this for He sees all our hearts and knows all our thoughts and all that we have done.

He spoke to the woman, and told her of the things she had done that did not please God. She thought He was a seer, to whom God told things that were not known to most folks. She said to Jesus, "I know that Christ is to come into the world, and when He comes He will tell us all things." "I am He," Jesus told her, "the One speaking to you."

Then the woman left her jar, returning hurriedly to the town, and said to her friends there, "Come and see a man who told me all the things that ever I did. Is not this the Christ?"

They went out and saw Jesus and asked Him to come into the town. He went with them and was there for three days. They listened to the things He taught them. They said to the woman, "Now we have faith in Him, not because of the things you told us, but because we have heard Him ourselves and know that He is the Christ whom God has sent down to us."

From there He went once more to the town of Cana. A rich man travelled from his hometown to ask Jesus to come and heal his son, who was sick. And the rich man said to Him, "Come as quick as You can, unless my child should die." Jesus said to him, "Go your way; your son is made well."

The rich man knew that Jesus would not say what was not true, and with a glad heart went back to his home. As Jesus drew near the house, the rich

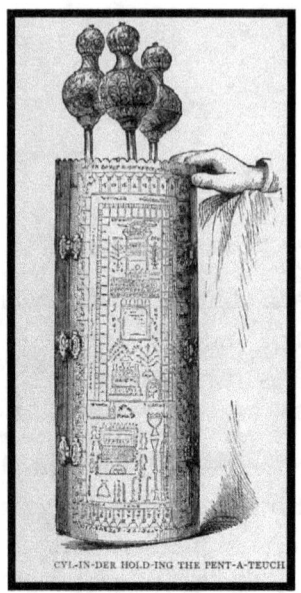

A Scroll

man's servants ran out to meet him and said to him, "Your son is well."

The rich man asked them to tell him what time the change took place, and they told him the hour that the fever left the lad. It was the same hour that Jesus had said to the rich man, "Your son is well." He and all those in his house felt in their hearts that Jesus was the Son of God.

The Jews did not yet know how to print, and they had no books like we have. They wrote with pen and ink on rolls of parchment made from the skin of sheep and goats. These rolls were called scrolls.

These scrolls were kept in the house of God, in a box or chest called an ark, and were brought out and read to those who came to the synagogue on the Lord's Day. The most important scrolls, all the books of the Old Testament, were kept at Jerusalem, but as all the Jews could not get there more than once a year, they had made rolls for their own use in each house of God.

Jesus came to Nazareth where He had been brought up and went into the synagogue, what the Jews called their church, on the Sabbath and stood up to read. He read from one of the old books where it was foretold that One should come to bring good news to the poor, to cheer the sad, to give sight to the blind, and to heal the sick. Then He closed the scroll and sat down. The eyes of all in the synagogue were on Him. He said to them that all these words had come true and that He was the Son of God, of whom the prophets wrote. They said, "Is not this Joseph's son? How then can He claim to be the Son of God?" They were angry with Him and led Him out to a steep hill on which their town was built, that they might cast Him down and kill Him. But Jesus got away from them, and they could do Him no harm.

## JESUS BY THE SEA

Jesus went on to Capernaum, and great crowds came there to hear Him and pushed so that there was scarcely room for Him to stand on the seashore. He saw two boats close at hand, out of which the men had gone to mend their nets. He went in one of the boats, which was Peter's, and told him to push it out from the land. Jesus sat down and taught the crowd from the boat.

When Jesus left, He said to Peter and Andrew, "Sail out to where the sea is deep and let down your nets to catch fish."

Peter said, "Master, we have been hard at work all the night, and not a fish have we caught. Since You told me what to do, I will let down the net."

When they had done this, they caught such a large haul of fish that the net broke. Then they called to their friends in the boat by the shore and asked them to come to their aid. They came, and there was more fish than the two boats could hold.

When Peter saw this, he fell down at the feet of Jesus and said, "I fear You, for I am full of sin, O Lord." Those with Peter were spellbound at the sight of the fish they had caught.

Jesus did this great wonder so that these men might see it and know that He was the Son of God, for they were to aid Him in His work and to go with Him from place to place.

The Wonderful Draught of Fish

Jesus said to Peter, "Fear not; from this time forth, you will catch men and not fish." He meant by this that Peter was to preach and to teach men that Jesus saves those who believe in Him from sin and from the nets that Satan spreads.

Jesus said to them all, "Come with me," and they had left their boats, their nets, and all that they had, and were with Jesus until the end of His life on earth.

On the Day of Rest, Jesus went into the synagogue and taught the folks there. In their midst was a man who was not in his right mind, and it was as if he were tormented by evil spirits. The man cried out to Jesus, "Let us alone. What have we to do with You, You Jesus of Nazareth? Have You come to kill us? I know You, that You are the Son of God."

Jesus said to the fiends that were in the man, "Be still, and come out of him." Then the fiends threw the man down, cried with a loud voice, and came out of him.

All those in the synagogue were struck with awe, and they said among themselves, "What does this mean? For He speaks to the fiends so that they are forced to do His will!"

When they came out of the synagogue, Jesus went to the house where Peter and Andrew dwelled, and James and John were there. Peter's mother-in-law was sick with a fever, and they told Jesus of it and begged that He would heal her.

Jesus took her by the hand, and commanded the fever to come out of her. She was made well at once, rose from her bed, and took charge of her house.

At the close of the day when the sun had set, great crowds came to the house where Jesus was and brought those who were sick and those who were not in their right minds, that He might cure them. He healed the sick, drove out the fiends, and would not let the fiends speak.

The next day Jesus rose before it was light and went out to a solitary place to pray to God. Though He was the Son of God, He had come to the earth in the form of a man and had all the needs that a man has. He had need of food and drink and felt pain and grief just as we do. He had need of man's help in His work and had need of God's help all the time. He knelt to God, just as He wants us to do, and asked God to be near Him, to give Him more strength, and to help Him to do His will.

When Jesus had gone, crowds came up to the house to seek Him. Peter, and the three disciples that were with Him, went out to look for Jesus. When they found Him, they told Him of the great crowd that sought Him.

Jesus said, "Let us go to the next towns that I may tell the good news there, for I was not sent to stay in one place."

He taught all through Galilee; His fame spread, and great crowds went to hear Him.

## JESUS HEALS THE SICK

A man came to Jesus and kneeled at His feet and said, "Lord, if You will, You can make me clean." This man was a leper. He had white sores on his skin and had to live by himself or with others who had the same disease he had. There was no cure for this man, who would be a leper until he died. It was believed that it was not safe to breathe the air near a leper, so he was sent at once out of the town, as soon as his case was discovered.

This leper must have heard of Jesus and the great works He had done, and the hope that had died out must have sprung up in his heart once more. If He could heal the sick and make the lame walk, why could He not cure him, so that he would be fit to live with those he loved? At least he could ask; oh, how great must have been his faith when he fell down at the feet of Jesus and cried out, "Lord, if *You* will, *You* can make me clean."

Jesus put out His hand and touched the man and said, "I will; be clean."

At once the sores left the man and his skin was white and smooth. Then Jesus sent him off and told him not to tell anyone who had made him well, but that he should go to the priest and do as Moses had told all those to do who had been lepers and were cured.

But the man was so full of joy that he could not keep it to himself, and he went out and told what Jesus had done for him.

Jesus Heals the Sick Man

# JESUS DOES GOOD WORKS ON THE DAY OF REST

Now there were some Jews who were known as scribes and Pharisees. They acted as if no one else was quite as good as they were. They knew all the laws of Moses by heart, and they were strict to see that no Jews broke those laws. A scribe is a type of person who writes.

These scribes and Pharisees were thought to be wise and good men, for they would fast and pray for a long while at a time and look as though they thought themselves too pure for earth.

But their hearts were bad and full of sin, and when Jesus told them they must give up their sins and lead the right kind of lives, they were angry with Him, and tried to make all the rest of the Jews hate Him as much as they did.

Jesus went down to Capernaum, and when it was known that He was in the town, great crowds came to the house where He was to hear Him preach.

Now there was a man who had been in bed for a long time and could not move his hand nor his foot. He had heard of the fame of Jesus, and it was the wish of his heart to get near Him that He might heal him with a touch. But Jesus was a long way off, and the poor, sick man could not walk one step. But he had kind friends, and they thought of a plan by which he could be brought near to Jesus, that he might at least hear Him preach.

So they took the sick man on his bed and transported him to the town; when they came to the house where Jesus was, the crowd was so great that there was no chance to get near Him. What were they to do?

Now the house was low and had a flat roof, with a wall around it, so that those who dwelled there could walk or sleep on it and have no fear that they would fall off. All the rooms downstairs led out into a court, which had a roof that could be slid off when it did not rain or there was need of fresh air.

So the friends of the lame man lifted the bed up on the housetop with him on it and brought him to the space in the roof, through which they could see Jesus and the crowds around Him. They lowered the man on his bed in the midst of the crowd, which had to make way for him.

When Jesus saw what great faith they had, He spoke to the sick man and said, "Your sins are forgiven." Some of the scribes and Pharisees who sat near said, but not out loud, "Who is this that dares speak in this way? None but God can forgive sins."

Jesus knew their thoughts and said to them, "Why do you think these things? Which could be said with the most ease, 'Your sins be forgiven you' or 'Rise up and walk?' But to show you that I have power to forgive sins, I will make him well." So He said to the sick man, "Rise, take up your bed, and go to your house."

The man rose, stood on his feet, picked up his bed, and went out and gave praise and thanks to God.

Those who saw him were amazed and said, "We have seen strange things today."

Now the Jews, as you know, were subjects of the Caesar of Rome, and to keep their peace with him they had to pay a tax. The men to whom they paid the tax were known as publicans. Some of the publicans were harsh and stern, and the Jews couldn't help but hate them. But all publicans were not so hard and stern. As Jesus went by, He saw one of these publicans with his gold and silver close at hand. His name was Matthew. Jesus spoke to him and said, "Come with me."

Matthew left it all, went with Jesus and, from that time on, did all that he could to spread the good news and serve the Lord Christ.

After Matthew became one of Jesus's disciples, there was a feast of the Jews, and Jesus went up to Jerusalem. Now there was at Jerusalem a pool, which was known as the Pool of Bethesda. There were five courts, or doorways, that led down to the pool. In these courts lay a great crowd of folks who were sick, blind, or lame.

This was the time of the year when an angel came to stir the pool. It was thought that the one who went first into the pool after the angel stirred it would be cured of all the ailments that he or she might have.

A man was there who had been sick for almost twenty years. Jesus saw him and knew that he had been sick for a long time. It saddened Jesus to think of it. So He said to the man, "Will you be made well?"

The man said, "I have no one to help me into the pool. When I try to get down to it, someone steps in ahead of me, and I am too late."

Jesus said to him, "Rise, take up your bed, and walk."

At once the man was healed, took up his bed, and walked.

Now it was the Day of Rest and the Jews, who were quick to find fault with those who broke the laws, said to the man when he came their way, "It is not right for you to move your bed on this day."

The healed man said to them, "He that made me well told me to take up my bed and walk."

They said to him, "Who told you that?"

But the man did not know and could not point Jesus out to them because the crowd was so great.

But before the feast ended, Jesus met the man He had cured and said to him, "Now you are well; sin no more unless a worse thing comes to you."

Then the man went out and told the Jews that it was Jesus who had cured him on the Day of Rest. For this the Jews sought to kill Jesus. But he told them that all of the works Jesus did were proof that God had sent Him and that He was the One of whom the seers had spoken of in the days that were past and of whom Moses had written.

He said that the time was near at hand when the dead should hear the voice of the Son of God and those who were in their graves should come forth. Then He would judge them. Those would be blessed who had done good, for God would give them a home with Him in the sky; but those who had done ill, and died in their sins, would not meet the smile of God, nor have a place near His throne.

Jesus said that if the love of God was established in their hearts, they would trust Him because God sent Jesus to save their souls from eternal death, which is separation from His presence in eternity.

Jesus and His five friends—Andrew, Peter, James, John, and Matthew—went out on the next Day of Rest and their walk led them through a field of corn. As the men had need of food, Jesus told them to pluck and eat the ears of corn, and they did so.

Jesus in the Cornfield

When the Pharisees saw Jesus's friends picking corn, they found fault, and Jesus told them that He was the best judge of what was right to do on that day; He was Lord of the Day of Rest.

In the course of a few weeks He went into a synagogue and taught on the Lord's Day. A man was there whose hand was so withered that he could not stretch it out or do anything with it. The Pharisees kept a close watch on Jesus to see if He would heal the man on that day so that they might find fault with Him.

Jesus knew their thoughts, and He said to the man with the lame hand, "Rise up, and stand where all can see you." The man rose and stood up.

Jesus said to everyone gathered, "I will ask you one thing: Is it right to do what is good or to do what is ill on the Day of Rest; to take life or to save it?" He stood and looked at all those that were in the place. Then He said to the man, "Stretch out your hand," and the man did so, and his hand was healed.

This made the Pharisees hate Jesus, so they went out of the synagogue and sought for some way to put Him to death. When He knew of it, He left the place and came down to the Sea of Galilee. Crowds came to Him from the land of Judah and from large towns that were far off to see the great works that He did. The sick crept near so that they could touch Him, and He made them all well.

# THE SERMON ON THE MOUNT

Jesus left the crowd and went to a lone place to pray to God. He spent the night there. The next morning, He chose twelve men that He might send them out to preach, to heal those that were sick, and to cast out devils. Their names were Peter; Andrew; James and John, the sons of Zebedee; Philip; Bartholomew; Thomas and Matthew; James and Lebbaeus; Simon; and Judas Iscariot.

The crowd was so great that Jesus went up on a hill, and the twelve went with Him. He taught them there. He told them that those who were in a high state of joy, with not a care, were called blessed. He said, not in these words, but in words that meant the same:

"Blessed are the poor in spirit, for God is with them."

By poor in spirit, Jesus meant those who did not think too much of themselves, who were neither vain nor proud, but were rich in love to God; He would be with them and bless them all their lives.

"Blessed are those that mourn, for their tears will be dried."

To mourn is to weep and to grieve. Jesus meant that those who wept for their sins would shed no more tears, for Christ had come to save them, and the good news should make them glad.

"Blessed are the meek, for the whole earth will be theirs."

Jesus meant by this that those who were fond of peace, and did not love strife, might live where they chose and would be blessed in this world and the world to come.

"Blessed are those who hunger and thirst for that which is good, for they will be filled."

This meant that those who sought to do right and to grow in grace had but to pray to God, and He would give them all the strength they might need from day to day.

Sermon on the Mount

"Blessed are those who are kind and good, for the Lord will be kind to them in their hour of need."

"Blessed are those who are pure in heart, for they will see God."

Those who are pure in heart will be fond of good works and will lead good lives, and God will not turn His face from them.

"Blessed are the peacemakers–those who try to keep the peace and to put an end to strife–for they will be called the children of God."

"Blessed are those who are ill-used for my sake, for the more the world hates them, the more God will love them."

Jesus told them that when men said unkind things about them for His sake, called them vile, and were harsh with them and full of spite, they were not to grieve but to be glad, because men mistreated the seers of old who told them of their faults and their sins and tried to lead them to Christ.

"Salt is good and gives a taste to our food."

Jesus told them they were to salt the earth. This meant that they were to tell the good news in such a way that men should want it and need it just as they did salt.

He told them, too, that they must let their light shine. He meant that they should let it be seen and known that they loved God and try to do His will. They were not to hide it from men, but to do such good works in Christ's name that those who did not love or care for Him might be drawn to Jesus–the light of the world.

Jesus said that if we do as we ought to do ourselves and teach men to keep all of God's laws, we will be called great in the place where God dwells. But if, like the scribes and Pharisees, we teach what is right and do what is wrong, we will not see God's face or live with Him on high.

He said, "You have been taught not to kill; he who puts one to death will be brought to the judge, and made to suffer for the crime. But I say to you that it is a sin to hate those who have not done any harm to you, and God will punish you for it."

Then He said that when they went to synagogue to worship God, they must try and think if they had done wrong, had been harsh, or had said what was not true. They were to go at once and do right to those whom they hurt in this way, for God did not care to have them bow down to Him if their hearts were full of sins they were not sorry for.

"We must be good and pure," Jesus says, "In all that we say and do: we must do no harm to those who harm us, but we must be kind and good to them, pray for them, and love them."

"Bless those that curse you and do good to those that hate you." This is a hard task, and none but those who have the love of Christ in their hearts can do it. But if we pray for strength, the strength is sure to come, and love takes the place of hate.

Jesus told the people they were to do right, not to please men but to please God. When they gave to the poor they were not to tell of it; when they prayed, they were not to choose a place where they could be seen of men–just to show how good they were–but were to go to their room and shut the door, that no one but God could hear them. Then God would reward them for their obedience to Him.

Jesus taught the twelve men how to pray, what words to use, and these words each child ought to learn by heart and use at least twice a day:

"Our Father which art in heaven, Hallowed be Your name. Your Kingdom come. Your will be done on earth as *it is* in heaven. Give us this day our daily bread. And forgive us our debts, as we forgive our debtors. And lead us not into temptation, but deliver us from evil: For thine is the Kingdom, and the power, and the glory, forever. Amen."

When they fasted, they were not to look sad as those did whose wish it was that men should see them fast, but they were to hold up their heads and wear a look of cheer that no one but God should know it. God would bless them for it.

Jesus said we must not want to be rich or to lay up wealth in this world, for when we die we cannot take it with us. But we should give our hearts to thoughts of God and strive to live so that we can share His home, where we will have more things to please us than all the gold in the world can buy.

Jesus said that no man could serve God and serve Satan too. We serve God when we do right, and we serve Satan when we do wrong.

So we cannot do the will of both God and Satan at the same time, and we must choose which one we will serve.

Jesus told the twelve men not to judge folks; He meant that they must take care how they found fault and blamed people. For they may not have done wrong, or if they did, they may have meant no harm. We cannot see men's hearts or know how they feel at the time they did the deed. But God knows all and may not blame them as much as we do. Jesus said that we should strive to do right ourselves, should see with clear eyes who did wrong, and have a right to tell them of their faults.

He said that what we want men to do to us, we must do to them. If we want them to be kind and good, and to treat us well, we must do the same by them.

He said, "Strive to go in at the strait, or narrow gate; for wide is the gate and broad is the way that leads to death." He meant that the good and the bad ways are like two gates in our path; one day we will have to choose which one we will go through.

The good way is small and hard to find, and we have to search for it with great care. But this path is one that leads to life and joy.

The bad way is like a broad gate that stands open and in plain sight. This wide gate leads down to hell, and crowds and crowds go that way, while few are found in the good way that leads to bliss.

Jesus said that at the last day some would call Him, "Lord, Lord," and say they had served Him and taught as He did. But He would say that He did not know them, for they had bad hearts and led lives of sin and were not fit to dwell with the good and pure in the home on high, where all is love.

He said that men were like trees. Good trees brought forth good fruit, but a bad tree could not bring forth good fruit. Men were to be known by their works, just as a tree was known by its fruits.

Then He spoke of two men, each of whom built a house. One chose to build on a rock. The rain fell, the floods came, and the winds blew and beat on that house, but it stood firm and the storm did it no harm.

But one of the men built his house on the sand. The rain fell, the floods

The Unfruitful Tree

came, and the winds blew and beat on that house; it fell with a great crash and was swept out of sight.

Jesus said that those who heard His words and did as He told them were like the wise man who built his house on a rock. Christ is our Rock. He stands firm. No storms can move Him. If we cling to Him, He will save us.

Jesus said that those who heard His words and did not do as He taught them were like the man who built his house on the sand. When the storm came on the last day, when God would judge the world, they would be swept out of sight. Oh, what a sad, sad day that will be for all those who have led bad lives, and done not the least thing to please God who took care of them and gave them all they had.

We must strive to be good all the time and to love Jesus, so that He will be near us and will take us home to live with Him when we die.

# GOOD WORDS AND GOOD WORKS

There was at Capernaum a centurion who had charge of one hundred Roman troops. One of his men, who was dear to him, was so sick that he was likely going to die. When the centurion heard that Jesus was there, he sent some of his servants down to ask him to make the sick man well. Those who brought the word to Jesus were Jews, and they spoke a good word for the centurion, who had been kind to them.

Then Jesus went with him. But as they drew near the centurion's house, the centurion sent some servants out to tell Jesus that he had not gone down to Him himself, for he was not good enough. Now the centurion sent word that he was not good enough for Jesus to come into his house. But if Jesus would speak the word, he was sure that the sick man would get well.

"For I stand at the head of my troops," said the centurion, "and say to this one, 'Go', and he goes; and to that one, 'Come', and he comes; and to the third, 'Do this', and he does it."

The centurion knew that if he could command his men like this, Jesus could do more and command all the ills to leave the sick man at the sound of His voice.

When Jesus heard these words, He was amazed and said to those who were with Him, "I have found no one who has such faith in men as this Roman. And I tell you that at the last day those

Christ with the Centurion

who have had faith in me will come from all lands, and have a place near God's throne; while the Jews, who will not put their trust in me, will be shut out."

Then the servants of the centurion went back, and they found the sick man to be well.

The next day Jesus went to the town of Nain. A great crowd went with Him. As they came near the gate of the town, they saw a dead man brought out to be carried to his grave. He was the only son his mother had, and her friends stood near her and wept.

When Jesus saw her grief, His heart was sad, and He said, "Weep not."

He came up to the bier, a framework for carrying the dead, and those who carried it stood still. Then Jesus said, "Young man, I say to you arise."

The man that was dead sat up and spoke, and Jesus gave him to his mother. A great fear came on all who saw it, and they

The Widow's Son Brought to Life

gave praise to God and said that a great prophet had been raised up in their midst.

In old times, those who lived in Israel did not wear shoes such as we do. They wore light soles, or sandals, which were bound on their feet with straps and thrown off as soon as they came into the house. Then water was brought for them to wash their feet.

Much oil was used in those lands, and is to this day. It was put on the hair to keep it moist and on the skin to make it soft and smooth. This oil, slightly firm, was called ointment, and was kept in a box and had a nice smell.

Now a Pharisee, whose name was Simon, asked Jesus to his house. Jesus went there, and they sat down to eat. A woman of the town, who had led a life of sin, when she heard that Jesus was there, came in with a box of ointment and bowed down at His feet.

She was full of shame, for her sins had been great, and she had come to Jesus to ask Him to forgive her and help her to lead a new life.

She wept, washed the feet of Jesus with her tears, and wiped them with the hairs of her head. She kissed His feet, and rubbed them with the ointment she had brought, and which had cost her a high price.

Washing Hands in the East

When the Pharisee saw it, he said to himself, "If this man had come from God, He would know what kind of a woman this is and would send her out of His sight."

Jesus, who knew every thought, said to him, "Simon, I have something to say to you."

And Simon said, "My Lord, say on."

Then Jesus said, "Two men were in debt to a rich man. One owed him a great deal, while the other owed him but a small sum. But they were both so poor that they could not pay him, and he told them to think no more of the debt, for it would be the same as if they had paid all they owed. Tell me now, which one of these would love him the most."

The Pharisee said, "I should think that he to whom he forgave the most."

Jesus said to him, "That is true."

And He turned to the woman and said to Simon, "See you this woman? I came to your house, and you did not bring water to wash my feet, but she has washed my feet with her tears and wiped them with the hairs of her head. You gave me no kiss, but this woman, since the time I came in, has not ceased to kiss my feet. My head with oil you didn't anoint, but she has poured her ointment on my feet. So I say to you that her sins, though so great, will be all wiped out, for she has loved me much."

He said to the woman, "Your faith has saved you; go back to your home in peace."

From this place Jesus went on through all the large and small towns, and told the good news that God had sent His Son into the world to save men from their sins. The twelve disciples were with Him.

Jesus might have been rich, for all the world was His, but He chose to be poor and to bear all the ills of life for our sakes, that we might be drawn to

Him and be saved from our sins. Good women, whom He had cured, gave Him such things as He had need of, and He did not lack for food or friends.

Jesus spoke at times in a strange way. He would take scenes from real life and paint them, as it were, with words, so that they were plain to all. These talks were meant to teach great truths that would lodge in the mind and stand out like scenes of real life. They were to take these truths and keep them in their thoughts from day to day.

One of these talks was of a rich man who had large fields and vineyards. When it was time for the crops to come in, the rich man found that his barns would not hold them.

He said, "What will I do? I have no room where I can put my fruits. This will I do: I will pull down my small barns and build large ones, and there will I store all my goods. And I will say to myself, 'You have stored abundant goods that will last you for years and years; take your ease, eat, drink, and be of good cheer.'

"But God said to him, 'You fool, this night you will die. Then who will have those things which you had saved for the future?'"

This story was to teach us that it is of no use for men to store up great wealth in this world, for they will have to leave it all when they die. It is a sin for a rich man to spend all that he owns on himself, to live at his ease, and to eat and drink, as if there were no poor in the world, and no God to serve.

Jesus told the twelve disciples not to fret because they were poor or to have the least fear that they might want for food or clothes to wear. "Think of the birds," He said. "They do not sow seed in the fields, nor reap grain and store it up for use in time of need. They have no storehouse or barn, yet they have all the food they want, for God feeds and takes care of them. If He does so much for the birds, how much more will He do for you?"

"Look at the flowers," Jesus said. "See how they grow. They do not work nor spin the thread to weave into cloth as men must do, and yet I say to you that King Solomon did not wear such rich robes as theirs. If then God gives such fine clothes to that which grows in the field like grass, and which in a day or two is burned up, how much more will He clothe you, even though your faith is weak to trust Him. So do not fret in case you will want for things to eat, to drink, and to wear because God knows that you have need of these things, and if you seek first to do His will, He will give all these things to you."

## JESUS AT THE SEASHORE

While Jesus was down by the sea, the crowd grew so great that He stepped into a boat and sat down to teach the people while they stood on the shore.

He said, "A man went out in the field to sow his seed, and as he threw the seed from his hand, some of it fell on the hard path by the roadside and the birds flew down and ate it. Some fell on the rocks and stones where there wasn't much earth, and it soon grew up on top of the ground. But the sun's warm rays made it droop, and as it had no root, in a few days it was all dried up.

"Some of the seed fell where thorns and weeds were and these took up all the room so there wasn't space for the seed to grow." The air and the sun could not reach the seed and soon it was choked to death.

"But some of the seed fell in good ground that the plow had made soft. The rain fell on it, the sun shone on it, and it sprang up and bore a large crop of grain."

The Sower

When the crowd had left Jesus, the twelve came near to ask Him what He had meant to teach by this talk of seeds that were sown here and there.

Jesus told them the seed was the good news that He came to preach. Those who preach or teach, sow either good or bad seed, which takes root in the mind or heart.

Some who heard Jesus's words wouldn't care for them, but would go on in their sins and feel no change of heart. New thoughts and fresh scenes would come and eat up the seed thoughts that Jesus had sown as quick as the birds ate up the seed sown by the roadside.

Some who heard Him thought of His words for a while and attempted for a short time to do right. But it didn't last long. This was the seed that fell in the midst of stones and sprang up at first but was all dried up in a few days.

Some would hear Jesus preach and were glad of the words that He spoke, but the cares of this world, this wealth, and the happy things of life were so much in their thoughts that they couldn't do the things He had taught them.

This was the seed that fell in the midst of thorns and the thorns grew up and choked the seed.

But there were some who heard Jesus preach and who attempted each day to do as He taught them. This was the seed that fell in good ground, which took root and grew and brought forth ten times as much as had been sown.

The Enemy Sowing Tares

One of the talks of Jesus was of a man who sowed good seed in his field. While the man slept, a foe came and sowed tares, or weeds, in the midst of the wheat, and then went on his way. When it was time for the wheat to grow up, the weeds grew up with it.

When the workmen on the farm saw the weeds, they went at once to the man of the house and said to him, "Didn't you sow good seed in your field? Where then have these tares come from?"

He said to them, "A foe has done this."

The workmen said, "Will we go out, then, and pull the weeds up by the roots?"

And he said, "No, because while you are pulling up the tares, you may also pull up the wheat with them. Let both grow until it is time to reap the

## Jesus at the Seashore

grain, and then I will say to the reapers, 'Pull up the tares first and bind them in stacks to burn. But put the wheat in my barn.'"

Jesus told the disciples what He meant by this talk of the weeds in the field.

The field is the world. He who owns the field and sows the seed is Jesus Himself. The wheat that grows up means those who hear His words and do as He has taught them.

The weeds are bad men who have no love for Jesus. The foe that sows them is Satan.

The time to reap the grain is on the last great day. The reapers are the angels.

Jesus will let the good and the bad live in the world until the last great day. Then He will send His angels to take the good to their home on high, but the bad will be cast out into the fire that is to burn up the world.

Then Jesus spoke of a man who went out to buy pearls. He went from place to place, and those who had pearls to sell brought them out for him to look at, but the man was difficult to please and bought few. At last he found one that was worth more than all the rest he'd seen. But its price was so great that he couldn't buy it. What did he do? Why, he went and sold all that he had and came back and bought this pearl of great price.

So will it be with those who wish to be rid of their sins and to be as pure as a pearl within. Jesus in us is the pearl of great price. Gold cannot buy it. But when we learn its cost, we should be quick to get rid of all that keeps Christ out of our hearts and make room for this one pearl, which is worth more than all else in the world.

The Parable of Nets

Then Jesus spoke of those who took their net and went out in a boat to catch fish. They cast the net out of the boat and threw it into the sea and when the net was full, they drew it back to shore. Then they sat down to sort the fish; the good ones were placed in their boats, and the bad ones were thrown away.

So it would be at the last day. The angels would come forth and sort the good from the bad. The good would be borne to their home on high, but the bad would be thrown into a fire that would make them cry out with pain.

Jesus said, "Have I made these things plain to you?" And they said, "Yes, Lord."

One of the scribes came to Jesus and said, "I will not leave you, but where you go I will go." Jesus said to him, "The foxes have holes in the ground, and the birds of the air have nests, but I have nowhere to lay my head." By this He meant that He was poor and had no place where He could go and lie down when He needed rest.

Stilling the Tempest

Night drew near and the crowd was so great that Jesus and the twelve went in a boat to cross the Sea of Galilee. There came up a great storm; the winds blew fierce, and the waves rose high and came with a great dash into the boat.

Jesus slept, for He was quite exhausted. The twelve disciples were full of fear and at last they woke Jesus and said, "Lord, save us, or we will sink."

Then He rose and spoke to the winds and the waves and said to them, "Peace, be still," and the wind ceased to blow and soon all was still and calm.

Jesus said to the twelve, "Why are you in such fear? How is it that you have no faith?"

As Jesus left the boat, an enraged man came out of the tombs to meet Him. He was so fierce that no man could bind him or tame him. He broke loose from all the ropes and chains, and no house could hold him. So night and day he would roam on the hills and in the caves or tombs, where graves had been dug and cry out and cut himself with bits of stones.

While Jesus was still far off, the enraged man saw Him, ran and fell down at His feet. He cried out, "What have I to do with you, Jesus, you Son of God? Harm me not, I pray you."

Now there was close by a great herd of swine. The fiends that were in the man begged Jesus to send them into the swine. Jesus said, "Go." When they came out of the man, they went in the swine, and the herds ran down a steep place and were drowned in the sea.

The men that fed the swine went and told what had been done, and great crowds came to the place where Jesus was.

When the people of the town saw that the angry man sat with his clothes on and in his right mind, they were in great fear. They prayed Jesus would leave the place at once.

When Jesus got into the boat, the man, who had been out of his mind, begged Jesus to let him go with Him. But Jesus wouldn't let him and said to him, "Go home to your friends, and tell them what great things the Lord has done for you."

The man went and told how he had been healed and those who heard him felt that Jesus must have been sent from God, for no mere man could do such strange things.

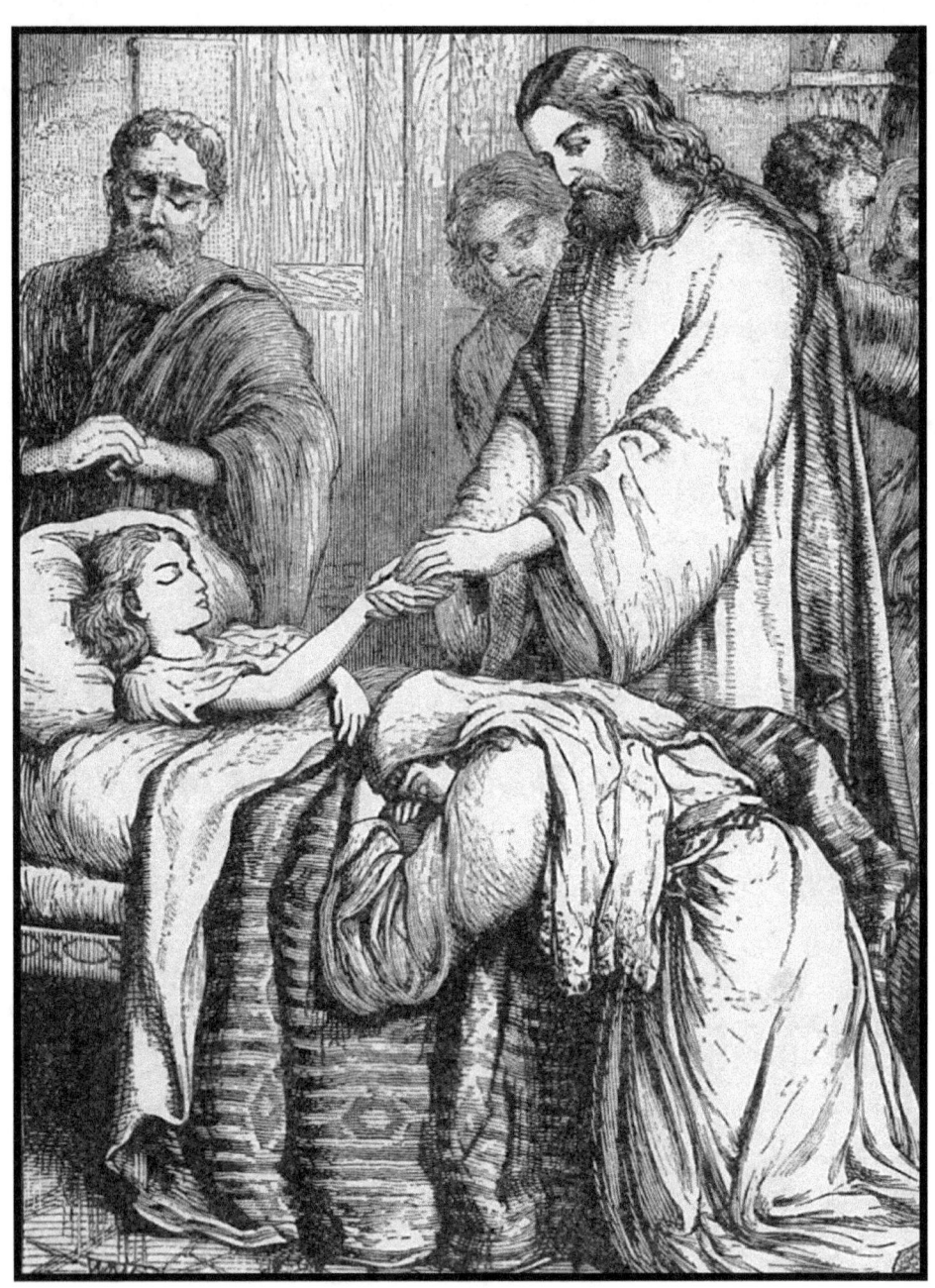

The Daughter of Jairus

## JESUS BRINGS THE DEAD TO LIFE

Jesus went back to Capernaum, and as He stood by the seashore, one of the chief men from the synagogue, whose name was Jairus, came to Him.

Jairus was in deep grief for he had but one child, a girl twelve years of age, and she lay sick at his home and there was no help for her. He said to Jesus, "My child lies at the point of death. I pray You come and lay Your hands on her that she may live."

Jesus went with Jairus, and so did the twelve disciples, and the crowd of people that had come up to hear Jesus preach. In the throng was a woman who had been sick for twelve years. She had spent all she had to try to be made well, but all the medicine she took did her no good, and no one could seem to help her. So she went from bad to worse.

When she heard of Jesus, she came up with the crowd at His back and put out her hand and touched the hem of His robe. "For," she said, "if I may touch but His clothes, I will be made well." As soon as she had touched Jesus's clothes, she felt that she was cured.

All this was known to Jesus, and yet He faced the crowd and said, "Who touched me?"

Peter said that someone in the throng had been pushed up close to Him, and thought it strange that Jesus did not know it.

Jesus said, "Someone touched me," and He looked around to see who had done it.

When the woman saw that Jesus knew all and that she could not hide from Him, she shook with fear, fell down at His feet, and told Him why she had touched Him and how that touch had made her well.

Jesus said to her, "Be of good cheer. Your faith in me has made you well."

While He yet spoke to her, there came a person from the house of Jairus who said to him, "Your child is dead."

When Jesus heard it, He said, "Fear not. Trust in me, and she will be made well." When Jesus came to the house, He found a great crowd there, who wept and mourned the loss of the young child.

Jesus said to them, "Why do you weep? She sleeps; she is not dead."

He meant that she would soon rise from the dead, as one who wakes out of a deep sleep. But mourners saw that she was dead, and as they had no faith in His words, they laughed at Him with disrespect.

Then He put them all out of the room except three of the twelve—Peter, James, and John—and the father and mother of the young girl. Then Jesus took the child by the hand and said, "I say to you arise." She rose from her bed and had strength to walk, and Jesus asked them to bring her some food that she might eat.

Her father and mother knew not what to think of these strange things. Jesus told them not to tell anyone about what he had done. There was no need for them to speak, for there was their child, well and strong, once more the light and joy of their house. Her parents' hearts must have been full of thanks and praise to God!

When Jesus went from the house of Jairus, two blind men came near Him and cried out, "Son of David, have mercy on us." They said this because they knew that He was of King David's lineage.

Jesus said to them, "Do you think that I can make you well?" They said to Him, "Yes, Lord."

Then He touched their eyes, and at once their sight came back to them. He said to them, "Tell no man what I have done to you." But when they left Him, they went from place to place and told all whom they met how Jesus had brought back their sight.

They brought to Him a man who was unable to speak because of the fiend that was in him. As soon as Jesus cast out the fiend, the man spoke. All those who saw it were amazed and said, "Such things as these have not been done before in the land of Israel."

But the Pharisees felt such hate for Jesus that they said that He could cast out fiends because He had the help of Satan, the prince of all fiends.

Jesus said to the twelve, "Come, let us go to some lone place and rest a while." For the crowds were so great that they had no time to eat. So they went in a boat quietly to cross the Sea of Galilee where they might rest and take the food they were so much in need of. But as soon as the folks heard of it they set out on foot and went by the shore until they came to the place where Jesus was.

When Jesus went out and saw them, His heart was moved, and He taught them and made the sick ones well.

When night came on, the twelve said to Jesus, "Send these off that they may go to the towns and buy food for themselves, for they have nothing to eat."

Jesus said, "They need not to. Give them something to eat."

Feeding the Multitude

They said, "Will we go out and buy bread and give it to them?"

Jesus said, "How much have you? Go and see."

When they knew, they said, "We have five loaves and two small fishes."

Jesus told the twelve disciples to have the crowd seat themselves in rows on the green grass. Then He took the five loaves and the two fishes and gave thanks to God for them. He broke the loaves and the fishes, and the twelve gave the food piece by piece to the crowd until all were satisfied.

When the feast was at an end, there was enough bread and fish left over to fill twelve baskets.

Then Jesus told the twelve disciples to get into the boat and go back to Capernaum.

When the crowd had left Him, He went up on a high hill to pray. When night came, He was there with none but God near Him.

The twelve were in the boat, out in the midst of the sea. Their oars were of no use, for the wind blew hard the wrong way, drove them back from their course, and made the waves toss the boat here and there.

Jesus could see it all from His high place on the hill, and in the night, He went down to the shore and walked out on the sea.

When the twelve saw Him, they were frightened, for they thought it was a ghost, and they cried out in their fear.

Jesus said, "Be of good cheer. It is I."

Peter spoke from the boat and said, "Lord, if it is You, ask me to come to You on the sea." Jesus said to him, "Come," and Peter came out of the boat and walked on the waves to go to Jesus. But when he heard the noise of the wind, and saw waves dash all around him, he was in great fear. As he felt himself sink, he cried out, "Lord, save me."

Jesus put forth His hand and caught Peter, and said to him, "O you of little faith, why did you doubt me?"

When Jesus and Peter came into the boat, the wind was stilled, and the twelve disciples were soon on the shore they had set out to reach. Then they fell at His feet, and said, "It is true that You are the Son of God."

As soon as it was known where Jesus was, crowds came from all the towns that were near and brought their sick in their beds that He might make them well. When He went through the large and small towns, they laid the sick in the streets and begged that they might touch but the hem of His robe. At a touch, they were all made well.

Christ Walking on the Sea

# JESUS HEALS THE SICK

Jesus went to Capernaum and taught the Jews there. But all that He said made them hate Him even more, and their chief priests did all they could to prove that He was not the Christ who was to save them. They thought that He who was to be the King of the Jews would come in rich robes with all the signs of high rank. So they could have nothing to do with a poor man like Jesus.

It made Jesus sad to have the Jews turn from Him, and He left them and went out to the towns of Tyre and Sidon, which were on the seacoast. No Jews dwelled there.

Yet a woman, as soon as she heard He was there, came out and cried to Him, "O Lord, You Son of David, come and heal my child, for she has gone crazy."

Jesus said He was sent to none but the Jews. This He did to try her faith, for she was not a Jew.

But she fell at His feet and cried out, "Lord, help me!"

Jesus said to her, "Great is your faith; your child is made well."

Then she went back to her house, she found her child had been made well at the same hour that she spoke to Jesus.

Then Jesus and the twelve went down near the Sea of Galilee once more. They brought to Jesus a man that was deaf, who would not speak plainly, that He might lay His hands on him and heal him.

Jesus took the man out of the crowd and touched his ears and tongue, and at once he was made well, so that he could hear and speak.

Crowds came to Jesus and brought those that were lame, blind, and deaf, and they all laid down at the feet of Jesus that He might heal them. Jesus healed them all, so that the crowds were amazed when they saw the man speak who had been unable to speak, the lame walk, and the blind see; they gave praise and thanks to God for what He had done.

# JESUS'S FORM CHANGED ON THE MOUNT

At the end of six days, Jesus took Peter, James, and John up on a high mount to pray. While Jesus was there, a great change took place in Him. His face shone as the sun, and His clothes were as white as snow and the light shone through them.

Moses and Elijah came to Jesus and spoke with Him.

Peter said, "Lord, it is good for us to be here. Let us make three temples: one for You, one for Moses, and one for Elijah."

While Peter spoke there came a bright cloud, out of which a voice spoke and said, "This is my dear Son, in whom I am well pleased. Hear you Him."

When Peter, James, and John heard it, they bowed down to the ground and were in great fear.

Jesus came and touched them and said, "Rise. Fear not." When they raised their eyes, they saw no one but Jesus.

As they came down from the mount, Jesus asked them not to tell anyone what they had seen until He rose from the dead.

The next day, when Jesus and His disciples had come down from the mount, there was a great crowd to see Jesus. One man knelt at Jesus's feet and said, "Lord, help my son. He has fits, and the fiends in him vex him so that he falls in the fire and in the water. I took him to those whom You taught to heal, to see if they could cure him, and they could not."

Jesus said, "Bring him to me." They brought the son, and he fell on the ground and foamed at the mouth.

Jesus said to the fiend that was in the young man, "Come out of him and vex him no more."

The fiend cried with a loud voice, shook the young man, and came out of him, but left him weak, like one dead. Those who stood near thought he was dead. But Jesus took the young man by the hand and raised him, and he stood on his feet and was well from that hour.

Then Jesus and the twelve went to Capernaum, and when they were in the house, Jesus said, "Why were you at such strife in your talk on the way?"

Ashamed, they held their peace because their talk had been as to which should have the highest place in the realm where Jesus was to reign as King of the Jews.

When they had sat down, Jesus said to the twelve, "He who seeks to be first will be last of all."

He took a child and set the child in the midst of them and told them that they must put pride out of their hearts and be as meek as a child. For he who thought not of himself, but did God's will as a child does the will of its father, the same should be great in the realm where Jesus was to set up.

Jesus taught there for some time and then set out for Jerusalem. The twelve went with Him.

When they were in Capernaum, those who took in the tribute money came to Peter and said, "Doesn't your master pay tribute?"

This was the tax the Jews had to pay to Caesar as the price of peace.

Peter said, "Yes." When Peter came into the house, Jesus met him and said, "Of whom do the kings of the earth take taxes? From their children or from strangers?"

Peter said, "Of strangers."

Jesus said, "Then are the children free. But in case we should give cause for blame, go to the sea and cast a hook and take up the fish that first comes up. In its mouth you will find a piece of money. Take that money and give it to them for me and you."

# THE GOOD SAMARITAN

Jesus went to the great synagogue in Jerusalem, and the Jews came there in crowds to hear Him preach and to find fault with Him.

A man of law stood up and said, "What must I do to be saved?"

Jesus said to him, "What does the law say? How do you read it?"

The man of law said, "You will love the Lord your God with all your heart, with all your soul, and with all your strength, and love your neighbor as yourself."

Jesus said to him, "That is right. Do this and you will be saved."

The man of law said, "Who is my neighbor?" Then Jesus spoke in this way, and said, "A man went down from Jerusalem to Jericho. And thieves fell on him, tore off his clothes, beat him, and went on their way, leaving him half dead on the ground.

"By chance there came a priest that way, and when he saw the poor man, he went by him on the other side of the road.

"Then one of the tribe of Levi came to the place, took a look at the poor man, and went by on the other side of the road.

"By and by, a Samaritan—that is, a man from Samaria—came that way, and as soon as he saw the poor man on the ground his heart was moved, and he instantly wanted to help him."

Now the Jews did not like the Samaritans and would have nothing to do with them. Those to whom Jesus spoke would not have thought it strange if this man from Samaria had left the Jew to die by the roadside.

Jesus continued: "The Samaritan could not leave the hurt man to die, for he had a kind heart. He went to the poor man and bound up his wounds, placed him on his own animal, brought him to an inn, and took care of him.

The Good Samaritan

"The next day when he left, he took out two pennies and gave them to the host and said to him, 'Take care of him; and if you need to spend more than that, when I come back I will pay you what you spent.'

"Which now of these three do you think was neighbor to him who fell among thieves?"

The man of law said, "He that was kind to him."

Then said Jesus, "Go, and do the same to those who need help. Go and do as the Samaritan did."

# MARTHA AND MARY

Jesus came to Bethany–a small place near Jerusalem–and a woman, whose name was Martha, asked Him to come to her house. She had a sister, whose name was Mary. While Martha went to get things and to cook, sweep, and dust, Mary sat down at the feet of Jesus to hear Him talk.

This did not please Martha, who felt that she had too much work to do; so she came to Jesus and said, "Lord, do you not care that my sister has left me to do the work alone? Tell her to come and help me."

Jesus said to her, "Martha, Martha, you are full of care and vexed about more things than there is need of. There is need of but one thing, and Mary has made choice of that which is good, and no one will take it from her."

He meant that Mary chose to care for her soul and to be taught how to live in this world, so that she might prepare herself for the next one. The one thing we all need is a new heart, full of love to Jesus and glad to do His work.

Martha and Mary

One of the twelve said to Jesus, "Teach us how to pray, as John taught those who were with him." Jesus taught them to pray the Lord's Prayer.

Then He said, "Which of you will have a friend and will go to him at midnight and say to him, 'Friend, lend me three loaves, for a friend of mine has come a long way to see me, and I have no food for him.'

"He who is inside will say, 'The door is now shut, and my children are with me in bed; I cannot rise and give it to you.'

"I say to you, though he will not rise and give to him because he is his friend, yet if he keeps on and begs hard he will rise and give him as much as he needs. I say to you, ask God for what you need, and He will give it to you. Seek and you will find. Knock and the door that is shut will open for you.

"For," He said, "If a child of yours should ask for bread, would you give him a stone, or should he ask for a fish, would you give him a snake? If you then, who are full of sin, know how to give good gifts to your children, how much more sure is it that God will give good things to those who ask Him."

Jesus chose seventy more men and sent them out, in groups of two, into all the towns where He meant to come, that they might heal the sick and preach the good news. They did as He told them and came back full of joy at the great things they had done through the strength that He gave them. Jesus told them that they should feel more joy that their names were written in the Book of Life—God's book—where He keeps the names of all those who love Him and do His will on earth.

The Feast of Tents was near at hand, and Jesus said to the twelve disciples, "Go you up to this feast, but I will not go now, for my time has not yet come." So He stayed in Galilee for a while. Then He went up to Jerusalem, but did not make Himself known unless the Jews should kill Him.

The Jews sought Him at the feast, and said, "Where is He?" There was much talk of Him. Some said, "He is a good man," and some said, "No, He is a fraud." But no one dared to speak well of Him out loud for fear of the Jews.

In the midst of the feast, Jesus went up into the synagogue and taught there. He said, "You both know me, and you know from where I came. I am not come to please myself, but to do the will of Him that sent me, whom you know not. But I know Him, for I have come from Him, and He hath sent me."

Then they made a rush for Him, but no man placed hands on Him because His hour had not yet come. God had set the time for Him to die, and no one could harm Him until that day and hour.

# THE MAN BORN BLIND

As Jesus came from the synagogue, He saw a man who had been blind from his birth. Jesus spat on the ground and made clay of the moist earth and spread the clay on the eyes of the blind man.

Then Jesus told the blind man to go and wash in the pool at Siloam that was near. The man went and did as he was told, and his sight came back to him.

His friends, and those who had seen him when he was blind, said, "Is not this he that sat and begged?"

Some said, "This is he;" and some said, "He is like him."

But the man said, "I am he."

Then they said to him, "How were your eyes cured?"

And he said, "A man, by the name of Jesus, made clay and spread it on my eyes and said to me, "Go to the pool of Siloam and wash; I went and did as He said, and my sight came back to me."

Then they said to him, "Where is He?"

The healed man said, "I know not."

It was on the day of rest that Jesus made the clay, and the Pharisees, when they heard of it, said, "This man is not of God because He does not keep the day of rest." They went to the father and the mother of the man who had been blind

"I was blind but now I see!"

and said to them, "Is this your son, who you say was born blind? How then does he now see?"

His parents said, "We know that this is our son, and that he was born blind, but by what means he now sees or who has cured his eyes, we know not. He is of age; ask him. He will speak for himself."

They spoke for fear of the Jews for the Jews had made it known that all those who said that Jesus was the Christ should be put out of the synagogue. So they said, "He is of age; ask him."

Then the Pharisees went to the man that was blind and said to him, "Give God the praise for we know that this man is a man of sin."

He said to them, "What Jesus is I know not, but this I do know: once I was blind, but now I see."

Then they said to the healed man, "What did He do to you? How did He cure your eyes?"

The man said, "I have told you before, and you did not hear. Why would you hear me say it once more? Would you be of His band?"

Then they spoke harsh words to him and said, "You do take sides with Him, but we stand by Moses. We know that God spoke to Moses; as for this fellow, we know not who sent Him."

The man said, "It is strange that you know not who sent Him, when He has brought sight to my blind eyes. Since the world was made we have not heard of a man who could give sight to one that was born blind. If this man were not of God, He could not have done this thing."

The Pharisees were full of anger and said to the healed man, "You have dwelled in sin from your birth and will you try to teach us?" The Pharisees pushed the healed man out of the synagogue.

Jesus heard of it, and when He found the man, He said to him, "Have you faith in the son of God?"

The healed man said, "Who is He, Lord, that I may put my trust in Him?"

Jesus said, "It is He that talks with you."

The man said, "Lord, I know that it must be so." He fell at the feet of Jesus, and gave praise to Him.

# JESUS THE GOOD SHEPHERD

Jesus said to those whom He taught, "I am the good shepherd. The good shepherd will give His life for the sheep. But he that is hired, and who does not own the sheep, when he sees the wolf will leave the sheep and run to save his own life. Then the wolf lays hold of the sheep and puts the flock to flight. He who is hired flees from the sheep, because he does not care for them.

"I am the good shepherd and know my sheep, and my sheep know me. I will lay down my life for the sheep.

The Lost Sheep

"Some sheep I have which are not of this fold; they too must I bring in. They will hear my voice, and there will be one fold and one shepherd."

The Jews found fault with His words and some said, "He talks like a madman."

As Jesus went out on the porch at one side of the great temple that Herod built, the Jews came round Him and said, "How long will You keep us in doubt? If You be the Christ, tell us so in plain words."

Jesus said, "I told you, and you have no faith in me. The works that I do, in God's name, are proof that I am sent from Him. But you do not trust me because you are not my sheep. My sheep hear my voice, I know them, and they go the way I lead. They will not be lost, and no one will take them from me for God gave them to me and no one can take them out of His hand. I and my Father are one."

Then the Jews took up stones to stone Him because He said that He was God.

But He fled from them and went out of Jerusalem to a place near the Jordan, where crowds came to hear Him and to be taught of Him. Many gave their hearts to Jesus and sought to lead new lives—to do right and to be good.

# LAZARUS BROUGHT TO LIFE

Mary and Martha, who lived at Bethany, had a brother named Lazarus, and he was sick. So Mary and Martha sent word to Jesus, but though He was fond of these friends at Bethany, He did not rush to go to them and stayed two days in the place where He was.

Then He said to the twelve, "Let us go back to Bethany for my friend Lazarus sleeps, and I must go and wake him."

Jesus meant that Lazarus was dead, and that He must go and bring him back to life.

But the twelve thought that He meant that Lazarus slept, as we do when we take our rest.

Now Bethany was near Jerusalem, and a crowd of Jews had gone there to weep with Mary and Martha. As soon as Martha heard that Jesus was near she ran out to meet Him, but Mary sat still in the house. Martha said to Jesus, "If You had been here, my brother would not have died. But I know that even now what You will ask of God He will give to You."

Jesus said to her, "Your brother will rise again."

Martha said, "I know that He will rise at the last day."

Then Martha went back to the house and said to Mary, "The master has come and asks for you."

Mary rose at once and went out to meet Jesus; those who saw her leave the house, said, "She goes to the grave to weep there."

As soon as Mary came to the place where Jesus was, she fell at his feet and said, "Lord, if You had been here my brother would not have died."

When Jesus saw her tears, and the tears of those who wept with her, He was full of grief and said, "Where have you placed him?"

They said, "Lord, come and see."

Jesus wept. When the Jews saw it they said, "See how He loved him." Some of them said, "Could not this man, who gave the blind their sight, have saved Lazarus from death?"

Jesus came to the grave. It was a cave, and a stone lay at the mouth of it. Jesus said, "Take away the stone."

Martha said to Him, "By this time he must be in a bad state for he has been dead four days."

Jesus said to her, "Did I not tell you that if you had faith you should see what great things God could do?"

Lazarus Raised from the Dead

Then they took the stone from the place where the dead was laid down and Jesus cried out with a loud voice, "Lazarus, come forth."

Lazarus came forth, bound hand and foot in his grave clothes, with his head tied up in a cloth. Jesus said, "Loose him and let him go."

Some of the Jews who came to be with Mary and Martha saw this great thing which Jesus did and had faith in Him that He was the Son of God. But some of the people went to the Pharisees and told what He had done.

The Pharisees and chief priests met to talk of Jesus and His deeds. They said it would not do to let Him go on in this way for He would raise up a host of friends who would make Him their king. That would not please the Caesar of Rome, who would come and take Jerusalem from them and drive the Jews out of the land. So from that time they sought out some way in which they could put Jesus to death.

As Jesus went out of the synagogue where He had taught on the Sabbath day, He saw a woman all bent up in a heap. She had been that way for almost twenty years and could not stand up straight.

Jesus said to her, "Woman, you are made well." He laid His hands on her, and she rose at once, stood up straight, and gave thanks to God.

The chief man of the synagogue was angry with Jesus because He had done this deed on the day of rest. He said to those in the synagogue, "There are six days in which men ought to work; if you want to be cured, come then and not on the day of rest."

Jesus said, "Don't each one of you loosen his livestock from the stall and lead him off to drink? If it is right to do for the animals what they need, is it not right that this woman should be made well on the day of rest?"

When Jesus said this, His foes hung their heads with shame, and all His friends were glad for the great deeds that were done by Him.

# THE FEAST AND THOSE WHO WERE INVITED TO ATTEND

One Lord's day, Jesus went to the house of one of the chief Pharisees, and while there, He spoke of a man who made a great feast.

When it was all spread out, the man sent his servant out to invite those to come in whom he had asked to the feast.

All who were invited cried out that they could not come. The first one said, "I have bought a piece of ground and must go and see it, so pray do not look for me."

The next one said, "I have bought five yoke of oxen and must go and try them. Pray, do not look for me."

The next one said, "I have just taken a wife and cannot come."

So the servant came back to the house and told his master these things. Then the rich man was in a rage, and he said to his servant, "Make haste and go out through the streets and lanes of this town. Bring in the poor, the lame, the weak, and the blind."

The servant did as he was told, and he came and said, "Lord, I have done as you bid me, and yet there is room for more."

The lord of the house then said, "Go out through the highways, and down by the hedgerows, and make the folks come in, that my house may be full for none of those who were first called will taste of my feast."

The man who spreads the feast is God. The feast is the good news: Christ will save us from our sins. The servant represents those who preach and urge men to come to Christ. Those who were first invited to the feast and would not come are the Jews. To invite the poor, the lame, and the blind to come

78  THE CONVERSATIONAL BIBLE

into the feast means that the poor and the sick are to be saved as well as the rich and the great.

Great crowds drew near to Jesus. He told them that though they might come and hear Him preach, if they did not care for Him in their hearts, they were not true friends, and they could not be His children. They must care more for Him than for all else in the whole world and must bear His cross–that is, they must do what is right, as Jesus did.

The Great Supper

# THE PRODIGAL SON

Jesus said, "There was a rich man who had two sons. One of them was wild and fond of feasts and happy times, but did not care for his home or the life that he led there. So he went to his father and said, 'Give me, I pray, my share of the wealth you have saved up for your heirs so that I may spend it as I choose.' The son took his share and went far from home and led a wild life.

"When he had spent all he had, there came a famine in that land, and he was in great want.

"That he might not starve, he went out in search of work, and a man hired him and sent him in the fields to feed swine. So great was his need of something to eat that he would have been glad to have had some of the coarse food with which the swine were fed, but none of the men gave it to him.

"Then he said to himself, 'The men my father hires have more food than they can eat, while I starve for want of what they can well spare. I will rise and go to my father. I will say to him, 'Father, I have done wrong in your sight, and in the sight of God, and have no more right to be called your son. Let me come back to your house, and be as a servant.'"

The Prodigal Son

"So the son rose and went to his father. While he was yet a long way off, his father saw him, ran and fell on his neck, and kissed his son.

"The son said to him, 'Father, I have done wrong in your sight and in the sight of God. I have no more right to be called your son.'

"But the father said to his hired men, 'Bring the best robe and put it on him, and put a ring on his hand, and shoes on his feet. Bring in the fattened calf, kill it, and let us eat and be glad. For this my son was dead and now lives; he was lost and is found.' Tears and sighs gave place to smiles and songs of joy.

"Now, the son who had stayed at home and kept his share of wealth that his father gave to him was at work in the field. As he came near the house he heard the joyous sounds and called one of the hired men to him to ask what it all meant.

"The man said, 'Your brother is here, and your father has made a feast, so great is his joy to have him back safe and sound.'" And the young man was in a rage, and would not go in the house; his father came out and coaxed him.

"The other son said to his father, 'For years and years have I been true to you and broke none of your laws. But you did not kill a fattened calf for me that I might make a feast for my friends. But as soon as your son, my brother, returned home after he spent your wealth in sinful ways, you killed the fattened calf for him.'

"The father said, 'My son, I have loved you all your life, and all that I own is the same as if it was my own; yet it was right that we should be glad and sing songs of joy, for this your brother was dead and now lives; he was lost and is found.'"

In this way Jesus taught those who found fault with Him, that God was glad to have men turn from their sins and come back to Him. He loved them in spite of their sins, and when they made up their minds to leave them and to do what was right, God met them more than halfway, and gave peace and joy to their hearts.

# THE PHARISEE AND THE PUBLICAN

Then Jesus spoke to those who were proud and felt as if no one else was quite as good as they were. He said, "Two men went up into the synagogue to pray. One of them–a Pharisee—chose a place where all could see him; he stood up and said, 'God, I thank you that I am not like other men. I fast twice a week, and I give to the aid of the synagogue a tenth part of all I own.'

"But the other man stood far off, bowed his head, and beat on his breast as he said, 'God help me and forgive my sins.' God forgave this man more than He did for the other. Those that are proud will be brought low and those who are meek will be set in a high place."

The Pharisee

Christ Blessing the Children

## BABES BROUGHT TO JESUS

Then babes were brought to Jesus that He might lay His hands on them and bless them. When the twelve saw it, they tried to keep them back and would have sent them away.

This did not please Jesus, and He said to them, "Let the children come to me and do not hold them back, for of such is the kingdom of God."

He meant that no one could have a home with God who was not as good, sweet, and pure as a young child, who hates sin and loves God with his whole heart. Then Jesus took the babes up in His arms, laid His hands on them, and blessed them.

As Jesus and the twelve disciples went on their way, Jesus told them that they were to go to Jerusalem that those things might be done to Him of which the seers and prophets spoke. He said that the Jews would beat Him and put Him to death, but that He should rise from the dead on the third day.

None of the twelve knew what Jesus meant by these things, but thought that He would set up His throne on earth and reign as kings do in this world and each one of them would have a place of high rank near His throne.

When it was known that they were to pass through Jericho, a great crowd came out to meet them. There was a rich man there who had a great wish to see Jesus. His name was Zaccheus. He was so small that he was somewhat hidden by the crowd, and he was in great fear that Jesus would pass without seeing him. Zaccheus ran on ahead of the crowd and climbed up into a tree where he could look down at this great man of whom he had heard.

When Jesus came to the place, He raised His eyes and saw him and said, "Zaccheus, make haste and come down, for today I must stay at your house."

Zaccheus came down and went with Jesus and was glad to have Him as a guest. There was quite a stir in the crowd, and the Jews found fault with Jesus and said that He had gone to be a guest with a man that was full of sin.

But Zaccheus told Jesus that if he had done wrong, he would do so no more, but would try to be fair to all men and to lead a good and pure life.

When Jesus saw that Zaccheus meant what he said, He told Zaccheus that God would blot out the sins of the past and help him to lead a new life. Jesus said that He had come to the world to seek those who had gone wrong, who were like lost sheep, to save them, and bring them to His home in heaven, where there was no such thing as sin or death.

# THE FEAST OF THE PASSOVER – THE SUPPER AT BETHANY

Now the great feast of the Passover was near, and a great crowd of Jews went up to Jerusalem to keep it. It had been kept since the days of Moses when God killed the firstborn of Egypt and passed over the homes of the Jews.

Those who were on the watch for Jesus to do Him harm said, as they stood in the synagogue, "What do you think? Won't He come to the feast?" For the chief priests and Pharisees had sent out word that those who knew where Jesus was located should make it known, that they might take Him.

Six days before the great feast, Jesus came to Bethany where Lazarus, whom He had raised from the dead, was. Some of the Jews knew that He was there, and they came not so much to see Jesus as to see Lazarus.

The chief priests searched for a way to put Lazarus to death while some of the Jews, when they saw that he had faith in Jesus, gave their hearts to Christ.

Jesus left Bethany to go to Jerusalem, and on the way the mother of Zebedee's children came to Jesus and begged that He would do one thing for her.

Jesus said to her, "What do you want?" She said to Him, "Grant that these my two sons may sit, the one on Your right hand and the other on Your left hand, in Your kingdom."

Jesus said, "You know not what you ask. Can you drink of the cup that I drink of and bear all that I will have to bear?"

They said, "We can."

Jesus said, "You will drink of the cup and bear the cross, but to sit on my right hand and on my left is not mine to give; God gives it to those who are fit for it."

When the other disciples heard Jesus's words, they were angry with James and John. But Jesus told them that those who sought to rule would be made to serve and that He came not to be served by men but to lay down His life for them.

Entering Into Jerusalem

When they came to the Mount of Olives, Jesus sent two of the twelve and said to them, "Go to the small town which is near you, and you will find there a colt tied, on which no man has ever ridden. Loosen him and bring him to me, and if you are asked, 'Why do you this?' say that the Lord hath need of him, and the colt will be sent at once."

The men did as Jesus told them, brought the young donkey, and put their robes on his back, and Jesus sat on him.

As Jesus went out on the road, the crowds in Jerusalem for the feast spread their robes before Him and covered the road with green branches from the palm trees. The people waved palm branches in their hands and shouted: "Hosanna to the son of David! Blessed is He that comes in the name of the Lord! Hosanna in the highest!"

This was the way in which the Jewish people used to meet and greet their kings, and they thought this would please Jesus so that He would pay them back when He set up His throne on earth. But most of them did not love Jesus in their hearts.

As Jesus came near to Jerusalem, He looked at the city and wept when He thought of the grief that the Jews were to know.

He taught each day in the temple at Jerusalem, but at night He went to Bethany to sleep.

One morning as Jesus was on His way back to Jerusalem, He saw a fig tree beside the road and went to it to pluck some of the fruit. But He found on it nothing except leaves. Then He said to it, "Let no more figs grow on this tree."

The next day when the twelve went by they saw that the fig tree was dried up from its roots.

They thought of the words that Jesus spoke and said, "How soon has the fig tree dried up!"

Jesus told them that they might do as much and more than He had done to the fig tree, if they had faith in God, and sought strength from Him.

Then Jesus told them a story: "There was a rich man who planted a vineyard, dug a ditch around it to keep wild animals and thieves away, made a wine press, and rented the place out to men who were to give him part of the fruit. Then he went off to a far land.

"When the time had come for the fruit to be harvested, the vineyard owner sent one of his servants to the men who had charge of the vineyard so that he might bring back his share of the grapes.

"But the men took the servant and beat him and sent him off with no fruit in his hands."

"Then the man who owned the place sent another man, and the bad men threw stones at this servant and hurt him so that he was near death. The next one they killed, and so things went on.

"Now the rich man, who owned the place, had but one son, who was dear to him. The man said, 'If I sent my son to them, they will be kind to him and treat him well.'

"But as soon as the bad men saw him they said, 'This is the heir; let us kill him, and all that is his will be ours.' They took the son, put him to death, and cast him out of the vineyard."

In Jesus's story, the vineyard is the world. The one who owns it is God. The bad men are the Jews; God had taught them His laws, and they had vowed to keep them. When they did not do it, God sent priests and wise men to try and make them do what was right. Stones were thrown at these men and many were slain.

At last, He sent his own dear son, Jesus. Now they meant to kill Him, as the bad men had killed the heir of the vineyard.

When the Jews heard this talk, they knew that Jesus spoke of them, and they were angry with Him and wanted to kill Him.

One day, on His way out of the temple, Jesus sat down near the box in which money was put for the use of the synagogue. He saw that the rich put in large sums. There came a poor widow who threw in two mites, which make a farthing, or the fourth of a penny.

The Widow's Mite

Jesus said to the twelve, "This poor widow has cast in more than all the rest. For they had so much they did not miss what they gave; while she, who was poor and in want, did cast in all that she had."

# PARABLES

A parable is a story of something in real life that will fix in our minds and hearts the truth it is meant to teach.

Jesus said the kingdom of heaven was like the master of a house who went out at morning to hire men to work in his vineyard.

The price was fixed at a penny a day and those who would work were sent out to the vineyard.

At nine o'clock in the day, the master went out and saw men in the marketplace who were out of work. He said to them, "Go to the vineyard, and I will pay you what is right," and they went their way.

He went out at noon and at three o'clock, found more men whom he sent to work in his vineyard. Later in the day, when it was near six o'clock, he went out and saw more men to whom he said, "Why do you stand idle all day?"

They replied, "Because no man has hired us."

He said, "Go you into the vineyard, and I will give you what is right."

So when night came, the lord of the vineyard had the workmen called in and each one was paid a penny.

Workers of the Vineyard

When the first workers came, they thought they would receive more pay than a penny. When they were paid for their work, it was just a penny, and they were unhappy and said, "These last only worked one hour, and you paid them the same amount as to us who have worked in the heat of the day."

The master said, "Friend, I do you no wrong. Didn't you say you'd work for me for a penny a day? Take what is yours and go your way; I have a right to do as I will with mine own. The last will be first and the first will be last."

Jesus also told them a parable of ten maids who went out to meet the bridegroom. For in those days the man who was wed brought his bride home at night and some of his friends used to go out to meet him.

These ten maids had lit their lamps and gone out to meet the bridegroom. But he did not come as soon as they thought he would, and as the hours went on they all fell asleep.

Now five of these maids were wise and five were not. The wise ones had brought oil with them, so that if their lamps should go out, they could fill them. Those who were not wise had no oil but that which was in their lamps.

At midnight those who were on the watch cried aloud, "Lo, the bridegroom comes! Go out to meet him."

And the five wise maids rose at once and went to work to trim their lamps.

The five who were not wise stood by and said, "Give us some of your oil, for our lamps have gone out."

But the wise ones said, "Not so, for we have no more than we need. Go and buy from those who have oil to sell."

The Foolish Maids

While the unwise maids went out to buy oil, the bridegroom came, and the wise maids went in with him, and the door was shut.

Then the five maids who had been out to buy oil came to the door and cried, "Lord, Lord, let us in."

But he said, "I do not know you," and would not let them in.

In the story, the bridegroom represents Jesus, who will come at the last day. The ten maids are those who claim to love Him and who set out to meet Him on that day. The oil is the love in our hearts, which burns and keeps our faith bright. We are to watch and wait for Jesus, for we know not the day nor do we know the hour when He will come.

Jesus came to the town of Bethany, and they made a supper for Him there. In those days they did not sit at their meals on chairs as we do, but lay down on a couch, as high as a table, so that they could rest on the left arm and have the right hand and arm free to use.

Martha, Mary, and Lazarus were there and while Jesus sat to eat, Mary came with a flask of rich oil that was worth a great price. She broke the flask and poured the oil on the feet of Jesus.

There were some there who found fault with this great waste, and Judas—one of the twelve disciples—said that the oil might have been sold for a large sum that would have done the poor much good.

Jesus said, "Blame her not. She has done a good work on me. For the poor, you have them with you all the time and you may do them good when you choose. But you will not have me always."

Then Judas went to the chief priests and said, "What will you give me if I bring you to the place where Jesus is, so that you may take Him?" They said they would pay him well. From that time, Judas was on the watch to catch Jesus alone.

Jesus began another parable and said, "There was a rich man who wore fine clothes and had great feasts spread for him each day. A beggar named Lazarus lay at his gate, full of sores; the rich man did not give him so much as a crumb. Dogs came and licked the sores on the beggar.

"The beggar Lazarus died and was born by the angels to Abraham's bosom. The rich man died and was laid in the ground. While in the pains of hell, the rich man raised his eyes and saw Abraham with Lazarus on his bosom and cried, 'Father Abraham, have mercy on me and send Lazarus that he may dip the tip of his finger in water and cool my tongue, for this flame torments me.'

"But Abraham said, 'Son, you in your lifetime had your good things while Lazarus was poor and had a hard lot. Now he has ease from all his pains and you are in torment. Between you and me, there is a great gulf; none can go from here to you, nor come from you to us.'

"Then the rich man said, 'My prayer is that you will send him to my father's house, for I have five brethren that he may speak to so that they come not to this place of torment.'

"Abraham said, 'They have Moses and the prophets, let them hear them.'

"And the rich man said, 'No, father Abraham; if one went to them from the dead, they will turn from their sins.'

"And he said to him, 'If they hear not Moses and the prophets, they will not turn from their sins though one rose from the dead.'"

A steward is one who takes charge of a house or land, pays bills, hires workmen, and is the master's right-hand man.

Jesus said, "There was a rich man who had a steward. Word was brought to him that this steward made a bad use of his master's wealth. So the rich man said to him, 'What is this that I hear of you? Let me know how you have done your work, if you would keep your place.'

"The steward thought to himself, 'What will I do if my lord takes my place from me? I cannot dig and am too proud to beg. I have made up my mind to do something that will put me on good terms with the rich so that they will not close their doors to me should I lose my place here as a steward.'

"So the steward sent for all those who were in debt to his lord, and he said to the first, 'How much do you owe?'

"The first man said, 'A hundred measures of oil.'

"The steward said, 'Take your bill and sit down and write *fifty*.'

"The steward said to the second one, 'How much do you owe?'

"The man replied, 'A hundred measures of wheat.'

"The steward said, 'Take your bill and write *eighty*.'

"The lord praised the unjust steward, for he thought he had done a wise thing."

Jesus said we were to use our wealth so as to make friends who will take us in their homes should we become poor.

He that is faithful in small things is faithful also in large ones. He that is unjust in the least is unjust in much more.

No man can serve two masters.

As Jesus drew near to Jerusalem, those who were with Him thought that the kingdom Jesus had described was close at hand.

He said to them, "A rich man had to go to a land far away, so he called his ten servants that he might leave his goods in their charge. To the first servant, he gave five talents. A talent is a large sum in silver. To the next servant, he gave two talents; to the third servant, he gave one. He said to them, 'Make good use of these gifts until I come back,' and then went on his way."

"Then he that had five talents went out and bought and sold and made five talents more. The one that had two talents did the same, but the servant who had one talent had dug a hole in the earth and hid his lord's money.

"When the rich man came back, he sent for his servants that they might tell him what they had done while he was gone. So the servant who had been given five talents said, 'Lord, you gave me five talents, and see—I have gained five more.'"

The Talents

"His lord said to him, 'Well done, good and faithful servant. You have been faithful over a few things, so I will make you ruler over many things; enter into the joy of the lord.'"

"Then the servant who had been given two talents said, 'Lord, You did give me two talents and I have gained two more.'"

"His lord said to him, 'Well done, good and faithful servant. You have been faithful over a few things. I will make you ruler over many things. Enter into the joy of the lord.'"

"Then the servant who had been given one talent came and said, 'Lord, I knew that you are a hard man and did reap where you have not sown and gleaned where you have not worked; for fear I should lose it, I hid your talent in the earth and here it is.'

"His lord said, 'You wicked and lazy servant. If you knew me to be such a harsh man, you should have loaned my money to those who would pay for its use so that when I came back I should have my own, and more with it. Take therefore the one talent from him and give it to him that has ten talents. For to him that has much will more be given; but from him that has not, all will be taken away from what he has. And cast you the useless servant into outer darkness, where there will be weeping and gnashing of teeth.'"

Christ meant to teach by this story that we were to make use of the gifts or talents that God gave us, and add to them as much as we could. Then when we die, God will say to us, "Well done," and invite us to share in the joy that our Lord has in store for us.

If we have but one gift, we must use that and serve God with it, or at the last day, He will take that from us, and we will have no part in the joy of our Lord.

Jesus said, "The good news is like a king who made a wedding feast for his son. The king sent his servants to call in those who were invited to the feast. But they would not come. Then he sent out more servants to urge more people to come to the wedding, but they made light of it and went their ways to their farms or shops, and some who were invited fell on the king's servants and killed them.

"When the king heard of this, he was angry and said to his servants, 'Go out to the highways and bring in to the wedding those you find there.'

"The servants did so and brought in both bad and good, so there was no lack of guests at the wedding.

"When the king came in to see the guests, he saw there a man who did not wear a wedding garment. He asked him, 'Friend, why are you here without wearing a wedding garment?' The man did not answer.

"Then said the king to the servants, 'Bind him hand and foot and cast him out because many are called, but few are chosen.'"

God is the king who made the feast for Jesus Christ, His Son, to which all are bid. The wedding garment we need is a true heart, which is full of love to Jesus. The good news is for all, yet Christ does not choose for His own those who think more of this world than they do of heaven, and they are lost.

Leaven

Jesus said, "The good news is like unto leaven or yeast, which a woman took and hid in some meal until the whole of it was light."

# THE LORD'S SUPPER

Now the day was come when the Jews were to celebrate the feast of the Passover. To do this each man took a lamb to the temple and killed it on the altar. The priest would burn the fat, but the man took home the rest of the lamb, and it was cooked. He and his family ate it that night.

The twelve disciples came to Jesus to ask Him at what place they should set out their feast for they had no house or home of their own.

Jesus sent forth two of them and said, "Go to Jerusalem, and there a man with a jug of water will meet you. Go to the house where he goes and say to the man who lives there, 'The master requested you to show us the room where He will come to eat the feast with His friends.' He will show you a large room, upstairs; there spread the feast."

The men did as Jesus told them, and the man showed them the room, and there they spread the feast.

That night, Jesus came with His twelve disciples, and as they did eat, Jesus said, "There is one here who will give me up to the Jews."

Now there was one of the twelve known as the one whom Jesus loved. His name was John, and as he lay with his head on Jesus's breast, he said to Him, "Lord, who is it?"

Jesus said, "It is he to whom I will give the piece of bread I dip in the dish."

When He had dipped the bread He gave it to Judas and said to him, "What is in your heart to do, do at once."

Now none of the rest knew why Jesus said those words. But as Judas had charge of the bag in which the money was kept, some of them thought that He told him to buy things they were in need of or give something to the poor. Then Judas went out of the house where Jesus and His friends were; it was night.

And when Judas had gone, Jesus said to them, "I will be with you but a short time. But before I go, a new law I give to you–the law of love. As I have loved you, so will you love each other, and by this all men will know you love Me."

Peter said, "Lord, where do You go?"

Jesus said, "Where I go you cannot come now, but you will be with me by and by."

Peter said, "Lord, why cannot I go with You now? I will lay down my life for Your sake."

Jesus said, "I tell you, Peter, before the rooster crows three times you will say that you do not know me."

As they did eat, Jesus took the bread, gave thanks, broke it, gave it to them, and said, "Take and eat."

Then He took some wine in a cup and, after He had thanked God, gave it to them, and they all drank of it.

He told them that when He was dead they must meet from time to time to eat the bread and drink the wine in the same way that He had shown them. As often as they did it they were to think of Him and the death that He died to save men from their sins.

# JESUS IN GETHSEMANE

Jesus spoke with them for some time. Then they sung a hymn, went from the house, and came to the Mount of Olives. They went to a garden there, known as Gethsemane. Jesus took Peter, James, and John with Him, and said to them, "Sit here and watch with me while I go and pray." He went from them a short way and knelt down and prayed. When Jesus thought how soon He was to be put to death for our sins, He was in such grief and pain that His sweat seemed like great drops of blood as it fell to the ground. God sent an angel to calm Him and give Him strength.

Christ in the Garden

When Jesus rose from His knees and went back to where His friends were, He found that they slept. He said to Peter, "Couldn't you watch with me one hour?"

He went off to pray once more, and when He came back, His friends still slept! He left them and came back a third time. Then He said, "Rise up, and let us go, for the worst of my foes is close at hand."

Judas Betrays Jesus

# THE JUDAS KISS

Now Judas had been on the watch and knew when Jesus went to the garden. Since it was dark, he thought it would be the best time to give Jesus up to the Jews. So Judas went to the chief priests and told them where Jesus was, and they sent a band of men out with Judas to take Jesus.

Jesus, who knew all things, knew that Judas was near, yet He did not flee.

Judas had told the band of soldiers that he would give them a sign by which they might know which one was Jesus. He said, "The one I kiss is Jesus; take Him and hold Him fast." Then he went to Jesus and gave Him a kiss.

The men laid their hands on Jesus and took Him. His friends who were near Him said to Him, "Lord, will we fight them with the sword?"

Peter who had a sword struck one of the soldiers and cut off his ear.

Jesus said to Peter, "Put your sword back in its sheath. Could I not pray to God to send to me a host of angels to fight for me and save me from death? But how then could the words of wise men come true?" Then Jesus touched the man's ear and made it well. Jesus said to those who took Him, "Have you come out with swords and narrow strips of wood as if I were a thief, to take me? I sat from day to day and taught you in the temple, and you did not harm me."

Then Peter, James, John, and the rest of the twelve disciples were in great fear and fled from Him.

The men that took Jesus led Him off to the house of the high priest, where the scribes and those who had charge of the temple had all met.

## PETER DENIES JESUS

Peter kept up with the crowd and went in a side door of the house to sit by the fire. One of the maids of the high priest came to him and said, "You were with Jesus." But he said, "I know not what you mean."

Then he went out on the porch and the rooster crowed. While there, a maid said to those who stood near, "This one was with Jesus."

Peter said once more that he did not know Jesus, and the rooster crowed once more.

Now it chanced that one of the high priest's men was a relative of the one whose ear Peter had cut off. He said to Peter, "Did I not see you in the garden with Him?"

Peter swore that he was not there and did not know the man. Jesus gave him a look as He was led through the courtyard where Peter was that felt like a stab in Peter's heart. Then the rooster crowed for the third time, and it came to Peter's mind what Jesus had said: "Before the rooster crows three times, you will deny me three times." Peter went out and wept as if his heart would break, so great was his grief and shame.

"Behold the Man!"

# CHRIST GOES BEFORE PILATE

Seventy men in the chief court of the Jews met in a room near the synagogue. The high priest and chief priests were there with the scribes and the head men of the temple. It was for them to say what should be done to those who broke the laws of Moses, some of whom had to pay fines or to be shut up in jail. But if a man was to be put to death they had to ask permission from the Roman governor, Pilate, whom the Caesar of Rome had set to rule in that part of the land.

It was night when the Jews took Jesus, and as soon as it was day they brought Him into court to have Him tried. The high priest said to Him, "Are You the Christ? Tell us."

Jesus said, "If I tell you, you will not think I speak the truth."

Then they said, "Are You the Son of God?"

He said, "You have said it."

Then the high priest tore his clothes and said, "By His own words we can judge Him. What do you say will be done to Him?"

They all cried out, "Let Him be put to death!"

They then spit in Jesus's face and struck Him with the palms of their hands. They bound Him and led Him blindfolded to Pilate's house, and told Pilate some of the things He had said and done.

Pilate said to Jesus, "Are You a king?"

Jesus said, "I am. But my realm is not of this world, else would my men have fought to set me free."

Pilate said, "I find no fault with this man." But the Jews were angry and cried that Jesus's words had made a great stir in all the land from Galilee to that place. Pilate said, "If He came from Galilee they must take Him to Herod, who rules that part of the land. Herod was in Jerusalem at that time.

When Herod saw Jesus, he was glad because he had heard much of Him and hoped to see some great things done by Him. But when Herod spoke to Jesus, Jesus said nothing. The chief priests and scribes stood by and cried out that Jesus claimed to be King of the Jews and the Son of God and had deceived men with false teachings. These were crimes for which He ought to be put to death.

Herod and his men of war made sport of Jesus and put on Him a robe such as kings wear, for Jesus had said He was a King. Then Herod sent Him back to Pilate.

Pilate said, "I find no fault in this man; nor does Herod, for I sent you to him; this man has not done anything for which He should be put to death."

Now it was the rule when this great feast was held, that one of those who was locked up in jail should be set free. At this time there was a Jew there, whose name was Barabbas; he had killed someone.

Pilate said, "Which one will I set free–Barabbas or Jesus, who is called Christ?"

While Pilate spoke, his wife sent word to him to do no harm to that just man, for she had had a strange dream about Him. But the chief priests urged the mob to ask that Barabbas be set free.

Pilate said, "What then will I do with Jesus, who is called Christ?"

They cried out, "Hang Him! Hang Him!"

When Pilate saw that he could not get them to ask for Jesus, he took some water and washed his hands in full view of

Pilate Washing his Hands

the mob and said, "I am not to blame for the death of this just man; see to it."

Then the Jews said, "Let His blood be on us and on our children."

But Pilate was to blame for Jesus's death because he gave Him up to the Jews that he might please them and keep the place that he had.

# ON THE CROSS

Now it was the law of the land that a man should be scourged before he was hung. So Jesus was stripped to the waist, and His hands were bound to a low post in front of Him so as to make Him stoop. While He stood in this way He was struck with rods, or a whip of cords, without any compassion for the extreme pain He endured.

Then Pilate's men of war led Jesus to a room, took off His robe, and put on Him one of a red and blue tint. Then they made a crown of thorns and put it on His head; they put a reed in His right hand. Then they bowed down to Him, as if He were a King, mocked Him, and said, "Hail, King of the Jews!" They spat on Him, took the reed, struck Him on the head, and beat Him with their hands.

The Crowning of Thorns

When Judas saw that Jesus was to be put to death, he was in great grief to think he had brought such a fate on One who had done no wrong. He took back to the chief priests the sum they had paid him and said to them, "I have done a great sin to give up to you One who had done no wrong."

They said to him, "What is that to us? See to that yourself." Then Judas threw down the silver and went out and hung himself.

Christ Carrying the Cross

Then the men of war took off the bright robe from Jesus and put His own clothes on Him and led Him out to put Him to death.

They met a man named Simon and made him bear the cross. A great crowd of men and women went with them who wept and mourned for Jesus. Jesus told them not to weep for Him but for themselves and their children, because of the woes that were to come on the Jews.

They brought Him to a place called Calvary, not far from the gates of Jerusalem. They nailed His feet and hands to the cross, which was then set up in the ground. All the while Jesus prayed, "Father forgive them, for they know not what they do." He meant that they did not know how great their sin was nor that they had in truth put to death the Son of God. With Him they hung two thieves, one by His right hand and one by His left.

Then the soldiers and the people mourning for Jesus sat down to watch Him, who hung for hours on the cross in great pain before His death came to Him. The soldiers took Jesus's robe and gave each one a share; for His coat they cast lots. At the top of the cross Pilate had put up these words: "Jesus of Nazareth, King of the Jews."

The Jews as they went by shook their heads at Him and said, "If You are the Son of God, come down from the cross." The chief priests and the scribes mocked Him and said, "His trust was in God; let God save Him now if He will have Him."

One of the thieves spoke to Jesus and said, "If You are the Christ, save Yourself and us."

But the other said, "Do you not fear God when you are so soon to die? It is right that we should die for our sins, but this man has done no wrong." After speaking to the other thief, he said to Jesus, "Think of me when You are on Your throne."

Jesus said to him, "This day you will be with me where God is."

Now there stood near the cross of Jesus his mother, and John—the one of the twelve most dear to Him. He told John to take care of His mother and told her to look on John as her son. John took her to his own home to take care of her and give her all that she had need of.

From the sixth to the ninth hour—that is, from twelve to three o'clock—the sky was dark in all the land. Jesus thought that God had turned His face from Him and cried out with a loud voice, "O God! O God! Why have You left Me?"

The Crucifixion

One of the men near the cross thought Jesus was in pain and took a sponge and dipped it in the gall, putting it up on a reed to His mouth that He might drink. Jesus wet His lips with the drink that was to ease His pain, spoke once more, bowed His head, and died.

Then the veil which hung in the temple, in front of the ark, was torn in half; the earth shook; the rocks were split; and those who, while they lived, had served the Lord, rose and came out of their graves, went into Jerusalem, and were seen there.

When those who had kept watch of Jesus as He hung on the cross saw these things that were done, they were in great fear and said, "There is no doubt that this man was the Son of God."

As night came on the Jews went to Pilate and begged him to kill Jesus and the two thieves so that they could be put in their graves, for it would not do for the men to hang on their cross on the day of rest. The men on guard broke the legs of the thieves to kill them, and thrust a spear into Jesus's side to make sure that He was dead.

Now there was near Calvary a garden, in which was a tomb in which no one had been laid. It was cut in a rock and was owned by the rich man Joseph of Arimathea. Joseph came to Pilate and begged that he might lay Jesus in this grave, and Pilate told him to do so. Joseph took Jesus down from the cross, wrapped Him in the fine linen he had brought, laid Him in the tomb, put a great stone at the door, and left Him there.

Laying in the Tomb

The chief priests went to Pilate and said, "It has come to our minds that Jesus said that He would rise on the third day, so we pray that you have men watch the tomb unless some of His friends come and steal Him and go on to say that He rose from the dead.

Pilate said, "You have your own watchmen. Go and make it as secure as you can."

So the chief priests went and put a seal of wax on the great stone and set men to watch by the tomb.

But that night God sent down an angel, and the angel came and rolled back the stone from the door and sat on it. His face shone like fire, and his robes were white as snow. The watchmen shook for fear of him, and had no more strength than dead men.

## JESUS LEAVES THE GRAVE

On the first day of the week as soon as it was light, three women who were friends of Jesus came to the tomb with the plants and spices they used to prepare those who had died for burial.

He is Risen!

They said as they went, "Who will roll the stone away from the door of the tomb?"

But when they came near they found that the great stone had been rolled away. When they went in the tomb, they saw an angel clothed in a long white robe, and they shook with fear.

He said to them, "Have no fear. You seek Jesus, who was put to death on the cross. He is not here, though this is the place where they laid Him. Go tell His friends that He has risen from the dead and bid them go to Galilee where they will see Him."

Christ Appearing to Mary

## JESUS APPEARS TO MARY

Two of the women from the tomb, with fear and yet with joy, ran to tell the good news.

But Mary Magdalene stood outside the tomb and wept. As she stooped down and looked in the tomb, she saw two angels in white, one at the head and the other at the foot of the place where Jesus had laid.

They said to her, "Why do you weep?" She said, "Because they have taken my Lord away, and I know not where they have laid Him." When she answered, she drew back and saw that Jesus stood near, yet knew not that it was He.

Jesus said to her, "Mary!"

She turned and said to Him, "Master!"

Jesus said, "Touch me not, for I have not yet gone up to my Father; go tell the brethren what you have seen and heard."

Mary told them that she had seen the Lord and all that He had said to her.

Jesus was seen two or three times on the earth after His death, and He came and spoke to those who were to teach and preach as He had taught them. But Thomas was not with the rest when the Lord came. When they told him that they had seen the Lord, he said, "I doubt it. But if I will see in His hands the marks of the nails and thrust my hand in the wound the spear made in His side, then will I know that it is He."

In eight days these friends met in a room to talk and pray. Thomas was with them and the door was shut. Then came Jesus and stood in their midst and said, "Peace be unto you." Then He said to Thomas, "Reach here and touch my hands, put your hand in my side, and doubt no more that I have risen from the dead."

When Thomas heard His voice and knew that it was Jesus, Thomas said, "My Lord and my God."

Jesus said to him, "Thomas, because you have seen me, you have faith in me. Blessed are they that have not seen me and yet put their trust in me."

More than five weeks later, Jesus met with these friends at Jerusalem. When He had talked with them He led them out as far as Bethany. Jesus raised His hands and blessed them, and as He stood, He went up in a cloud out of their sight.

When the day of Pentecost, or harvest feast, had come, Peter and the rest of those whom Jesus had taught were all in one place.

All at once there came the great rush of a strong wind that filled the room where they were. Tongues of fire came down on each one of them, their hearts were filled with a strange power, and they spoke all known languages.

There were men there from all parts of the East, and when they heard these men of Galilee speak in their own tongues of the works of God, they were amazed. Some said, "These men are full of new wine."

But Peter stood up and said the men were not drunk, but that this strange gift of speech was one of the signs that God had told the Jews that He would send on the earth. Peter preached so well to the crowd that many left the ranks of sin, gave their hearts to Christ, and did good works.

From that time, those who had been taught by Jesus while He was on earth went out to teach and preach the good news. They gave alms to the poor, healed the sick, and did all the good that they could.

# STEPHEN IS KILLED BY STONING

One of them, named Stephen, stood up to preach and to tell the Jews what God had done for them, and to try to make them give up their sins. He spoke in plain words and said, "The Jews of old put to death those who were sent to tell them that Jesus was to come; now you have slain the Just One Himself."

When the Jews heard Stephen's words, they were full of rage and gnashed their teeth at him like wild beasts. But he raised his eyes to the sky and saw a great light there. He said, "I see Jesus at the right hand of God."

Then they cried out with a loud voice and held their hand over their ears so that they could not hear Stephen's words; they brought him out of the town to kill him with stones.

Stephen knelt down and asked God to forgive them for this sin. Then he died.

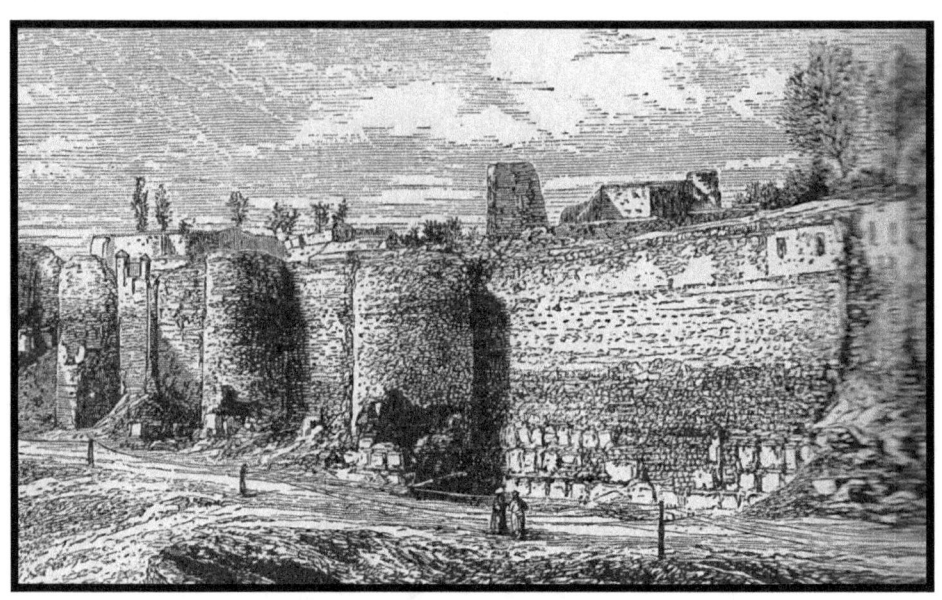

Houses on the Walls of Damascus

# PAUL'S LIFE, SHIPWRECK, AND DEATH

The men who threw the stones at Stephen took off their cloaks, that they might have the free use of their arms, and laid them at the feet of a young man named Saul.

Now Saul had done much harm to the good cause and was in a great rage with those who were friends of Jesus and taught His truths. So Saul went to the high priest at Jerusalem and asked to be sent to Damascus, so that if he found friends of Jesus there he might bind them with cords and bring them back to Jerusalem. The high priest gave him notes to those who had charge of the synagogues in Damascus, and he set out for that place. But when Saul came near the town there shone round him a great light, and he was in such fear that he fell to the ground. A voice said to him, "Saul, Saul, why do you hate me and hunt me down?"

Saul said, "Who are You, Lord?"

The voice said, "I am Jesus, whom you do use so ill."

Then Saul shook with fear and said, "Lord, what will You have me to do?"

The Lord said, "Rise, and go into the town, and it will be shown to you what you must do." And the men who were with Saul stood dazed and speechless, for they heard the voice but could see no man.

When Saul rose from the earth he could not see, for the light had made him blind; those who were with him led him by the hand into Damascus. For three days, he had no sight; he could not eat nor drink.

But God sent Ananias, a different man than the one who was married to Sapphira, a good man, to touch Saul's eyes and his sight and his strength came back. His heart was changed, and there was no man who could preach as Paul did, by which name he was now known.

For a while, Paul traveled with Barnabas. Then Paul took Silas with him, and they made both friends and foes. The Jews at Philippi found fault with them, beat them, put them in jail, and told the jailer to keep them safe. So the jailer put their feet securely in the stocks–which were great blocks of wood with holes in them.

At midnight, Paul and Silas prayed, and those in the jail heard them. Then all at once there came a great earthquake which shook the jail, and the doors flew open, and the chains fell from those who were bound. The jailer woke from his sleep, and when he saw that all the prison doors had opened, he feared he would be put to death if those in the jail had fled. So he drew his sword to kill himself. But Paul cried to him with a loud voice, "Do yourself no harm, for we are all here."

Then the jailer brought a light, and came to the cell where Paul and Silas were, and he knelt there and cried out, "Sirs, what must I do to be saved?"

They said, "Have faith in the Lord Jesus Christ, and you will be saved."

That same hour of the night the jailer took Paul and Silas and washed their wounds and brought them food. His heart was full of joy; he and all in his house were made Christians, and God forgave their past sins.

The next morning, the chief man at Philippi sent word to the jailer to let those men go, for the Jews found they had no right to beat Paul. They feared the law and begged Paul and Silas to leave the town.

Paul went to Athens, the chief town of Greece, which was full of false gods to whom altars had been built. But there was one altar, on which were the words, "TO AN UNKNOWN GOD."

Those who built it felt that there was one God of whom they had not been taught, and this altar was for Him.

Paul taught in Athens, both indoors and outdoors. When the wise men heard that he told of Jesus, and that we were all to rise from the dead, they brought him to Areopagus, where the chief court was held. They said to Paul, "Tell us now what the good news is. For you speak strange words, and we would like to understand the meaning of those words."

Paul told them that there was but one true God, and they must serve Him, give up their sins, and put their trust in Jesus, and they would all be saved at the last day.

## Paul's Life, Shipwreck, and Death

Then Paul went to Corinth where he spent some time. At the end of many years he came back to Jerusalem. The Lord's friends met him, and were glad to see his face once more. He told them where he had been and how God had helped him.

Paul Leaving Tyre

Paul went up to the synagogue. While he was there, some Jews from Asia saw him, took hold of him, and cried out, "Men of Israel, help us. This is the man who has taught that we were not to do as Moses told us, nor to come here to pay our vows. He has brought with him gentiles whom it is a crime to let come into our temple."

Soon all the town was in an uproar and Paul was brought into the synagogue, and the gates that led to the courts were all shut. As they were about to kill him, someone went and told the chief who had charge of a band of Roman troops and dwelt near the great synagogue to guard it. The chief and some of his men ran down in the midst of the crowd, who, as soon as they saw them, ceased to beat Paul.

The chief took Paul from them, had him bound with chains, and asked who he was and what he had done. Some cried this, and some that, but no one could tell just what they said.

The chief led Paul off to his own house to save Paul's life, and the mob brought up the rear and cried out, "Away with him! Kill him!" The next day the chief let Paul go, and sent him to Felix, who ruled in Judea. Here he was shut up in jail and was there for two years or more. He told them who he was, why he had gone to Jerusalem, and said he had done no wrong that he knew of; though some might say it was wrong for him to preach that the dead should rise from their graves at the last day.

Felix sent the Jews off and requested the jailer let Paul walk in and out as he chose and see all the friends who might call. He was there for two years, and at the end of that time, Porcius Festus took Felix's place as ruler of Judea.

At last Paul was sent to Rome to be tried before the Caesar. While on the sea a fierce wind sprang up and beat the ship so that the men could not steer. They were in great fear of drowning. But Paul told them not to fear, for though the ship might be a wreck there would be no loss of life. At the end of two weeks the ship struck the isle of Malta, and the men swam to the shore on bits of boards.

Paul stayed here for three months, and then went to Rome, where he dwelled for two years or more and taught men to trust in the Lord and to do right.

We are not told when or how he died.

Paul Preaching

# WHAT JOHN SAW WHILE ON THE ISLE OF PATMOS

John wrote the last book in the New Testament. It is called Revelation, which means that it tells what no one else but John knew.

John was sent to the lone isle of Patmos by one of the bad Emperors of Rome, who would not let him preach or teach the truths that Christ taught.

Patmos

While he was at Patmos, Jesus came to him in a dream and showed John all the things that he wrote of in this book.

John said, "I heard a great voice like a trumpet, and as I turned to see who it was that spoke to me, I saw Jesus clothed in a robe that fell to His feet and was held at the waist by a belt of gold. When I saw Him, I fell at His feet like one dead. He laid His right hand on me and said, 'Fear not; I am He who died on the cross, but who now lives to die no more.'"

Jesus told John to write all that he saw and to send it to the churches for which it was meant.

Then John saw a door open in the sky, and a voice said to him, "Come up here, and I will show you what will take place in the time to come." John heard the angels sing songs of praise to Jesus, whom they called the Lamb that was slain. John was shown strange things that were to teach him what the friends of Christ would have to put up with until the end of the world. He was shown, too, how the Lord would save God's people from their foes, so that at last no one could hurt or harm them.

# THE GREAT WHITE THRONE

Then John saw a great white throne in heaven, and Jesus sat on it. The dead rose from their graves and came and stood near the throne to be judged. All the things that they had done while on the earth were put down in the books out of which they were judged. If their names were not in the Book of Life, they were cast into the lake of fire.

When this great day was past, John saw new skies and a new earth, for the old earth and skies had burned up. He saw the New Jerusalem come down from the skies and heard a voice say that God would come and live with men.

John's Vision

# THE LAND OF LIGHT

Round the New Jerusalem, which was built of gold, was a high wall with twelve gates, three on each side. At each gate was an angel to guard it. In the walls were all kinds of rich and rare gems, and its twelve gates were made of pearls.

There was no need of the sun or the moon, for God was there and Jesus, and they made it light. Those whom Jesus had saved—Jews and Gentiles, rich and poor—were to come and live in it. The gates should not be shut, for there will be no night there. None but those whose names are in the Book of Life will go into it.

John saw a pure river called the water of life. On each side of it grew the tree of life that bore twelve kinds of fruit, which were ripe each month. Those who dwell in that land of light, eat the fruits of the tree of life, and drink of the water of life will see the Lord's face and be with Him and serve Him.

He will wipe all tears from their eyes, and there will be no more death, nor grief, nor pain.

Jesus said to John, "Blessed are they who keep God's laws and do His will that they may pass through the gates to His bright home on high."

# INDEX OF ILLUSTRATIONS

| | | | |
|---|---|---|---|
| The Nativity | 12 | "I was Blind but Now I See!" | 69 |
| The Annunciation | 14 | The Lost Sheep | 71 |
| Simeon in the Temple | 16 | Lazarus Raised from the Dead | 74 |
| The Guiding Star | 18 | The Great Supper | 78 |
| Wise Men Bringing Gifts | 20 | The Prodigal Son | 79 |
| Jesus in the Temple | 22 | The Pharisee | 81 |
| John the Baptist | 24 | Christ Blessing the Children | 82 |
| The Baptism of Christ | 26 | Entering into Jerusalem | 86 |
| Driving out the Sellers | 28 | The Widow's Mite | 88 |
| The Woman at the Well | 30 | Workers of the Vineyard | 89 |
| A Scroll | 32 | The Foolish Maids | 90 |
| The Wonderful Draught of Fish | 33 | The Talents | 93 |
| Jesus Heals the Sick Man | 36 | Leaven | 94 |
| Jesus in the Cornfield | 40 | Christ in the Garden | 97 |
| Sermon on the Mount | 42 | Judas Betrays Jesus | 98 |
| The Unfruitful Tree | 45 | "Behold the Man!" | 102 |
| Christ with the Centurion | 47 | Pilate Washing his Hands | 104 |
| The Widow's Son Brought to Life | 48 | The Crowning of Thorns | 105 |
| Washing Hands in the East | 49 | Christ Carrying the Cross | 106 |
| The Sower | 51 | The Crucifixion | 108 |
| The Enemy Sowing Tares | 52 | Laying in the Tomb | 109 |
| The Parable of Nets | 53 | He is Risen! | 111 |
| Stilling the Tempest | 54 | Christ Appearing to Mary | 112 |
| The Daughter of Jairus | 56 | Houses on the Walls of Damascus | 116 |
| Feeding the Multitude | 59 | Paul Leaving Tyre | 119 |
| Christ Walking on the Sea | 60 | Paul Preaching | 120 |
| The Good Samaritan | 66 | Patmos | 121 |
| Martha and Mary | 67 | John's Vision | 124 |

# BIBLIOGRAPHY

*History of the New Testament in Words of One Syllable* by Josephine Pollard. Copyright © 1888 by Joseph L. Blamire, George Routledge and Sons, New York: 9 Lafayette Place; London: Broadway, Ludgate Hill.

HCSB Study Bible, Holman Christian Standard Bible (2010). Nashville, TN: Holman Bible Publishers.

For more information about
**Angela Scott**
&
*The Conversational Bible*

please visit:

*www.thatstorylady.com*
*angelascott@thatstorylady.com*
*Twitter: @angelascott*
*www.facebook.com/TheConversationalBible*

For more information about
AMBASSADOR INTERNATIONAL
please visit:

*www.ambassador-international.com*
*@AmbassadorIntl*
*www.facebook.com/AmbassadorIntl*

www.ingramcontent.com/pod-product-compliance
Lightning Source LLC
LaVergne TN
LVHW051600080426
835510LV00020B/3067